Isaac C. Parker

THE OKLAHOMA WESTERN BIOGRAPHIES
RICHARD W. ETULAIN, GENERAL EDITOR

Isaac C. Parker

Federal Justice on the Frontier

Michael J. Brodhead

UNIVERSITY OF OKLAHOMA PRESS : NORMAN

Also by Michael J. Brodhead

Persevering Populist: The Life of Frank Doster (Reno, 1969)
A Soldier-Scientist in the American Southwest (Tucson, 1973)
(with Paul Russell Cutright) *Elliott Coues: Naturalist and Frontier Historian* (Urbana, 1981)
(with James C. McCormick) *Brushwork Diary: Watercolors of Early Nevada* (Reno, 1991)
(ed., with John S. Tomer) *A Naturalist in Indian Territory: The Journals of S. W. Woodhouse* (Norman, 1992)
David J. Brewer: The Life of a Supreme Court Justice, 1837–1910 (Carbondale, Ill., 1994)

Publication of this book is made possible through the generosity of Edith Kinney Gaylord.

Library of Congress Cataloging-in-Publication Data

Brodhead, Michael J.
    Isaac C. Parker : federal justice on the frontier / Michael J. Brodhead.
        p. cm.—(The Oklahoma western biographies ; v. 20)
    Includes bibliographical references and index.
    1. Parker, Isaac Charles, 1838–1896.   2. Judges—Arkansas—Biography.   3. Judges—Oklahoma—Biography.   4. Criminal justice, Administration of—Oklahoma—History.   I. Title.   II. Series.

KF368.P32 B76 2003
347.73'14'092—dc21
[B]   2002031986

Isaac C. Parker: Federal Justice on the Frontier is Volume 20 in The Oklahoma Western Biographies.

The paper in this book meets the guidelines for permanence and durability of the Committee on Production Guidelines for Book Longevity of the Council on Library Resources, Inc. ∞

1   2   3   4   5   6   7   8   9   10

For my sons, Lynus and John

Contents

Illustrations

Series Editor's Preface

STORIES of heroes and heroines have intrigued many generations of listeners and readers. Americans, like people everywhere, have been captivated by the lives of military, political, and religious figures and of intrepid explorers, pioneers, and rebels. The Oklahoma Western Biographies endeavor to build on this fascination with biography and to link it with two other abiding interests of Americans: the frontier and the American West. Although volumes in the series carry no notes, they are prepared by leading scholars, are soundly researched, and include a list of sources used. Each volume is a lively synthesis based on thorough examination of pertinent primary and secondary sources.

Above all, The Oklahoma Western Biographies aim at two goals: to provide readable life stories of significant westerners and to show how their lives illuminate a notable topic, an influential movement, or a series of important events in the history and culture of the American West.

Michael J. Brodhead's new biography of Isaac C. Parker (1838–1896) provides a thorough study of the nationally recognized judge's twenty-year career in the courts of Arkansas. As Brodhead demonstrates, Parker became a major figure in the legal history of the American West. Throughout this superbly researched and clearly organized life story, the author furnishes valuable discussions of Parker's important decisions in his career from 1875 to 1896 as a federal judge in Fort Smith, Arkansas.

Readers will benefit particularly from Brodhead's close examination of Parker's undeserved reputation as the

Hanging Judge. The author proves that Parker did not merit this misappellation. True, he often imposed death penalties, but those sentences were almost always for the capital crimes of murder or rape, for which the accepted penalty was death. Most of all, Brodhead repeatedly shows, Judge Parker sympathized with victims and their families, who were often innocent bystanders facing cowardly and violent criminals.

Brodhead paints a full, rounded portrait of Parker. On the one hand, the author details the judge's strengths: his devotion to his work, his balanced treatment of minority groups and women, and his unwillingness to deviate from accepted legal and court procedures. On the other, Brodhead also treats the darker side of Parker's character and career: his tendency to denigrate his outspoken opponents, to attack verbally those who dissented from his decisions, and to become embroiled in endless arguments on minor or tangential points. Brodhead also deals at length with the judge's moral views, his community activities, and his personal life.

In short, this important book on Isaac C. Parker fulfills the twin purposes of The Oklahoma Western Biographies series. It is a clear, readable biography of a notable western figure, and it clarifies how Judge Parker's life and career illuminate larger themes in the history of the American West.

RICHARD W. ETULAIN

University of New Mexico

Acknowledgments

THE author received much-needed help in matters of the law from attorneys. I am especially grateful for the wise and generous counsel of James Smith and Marshall Smith. Others learned in the law who also supplied assistance were Felix F. Stumph, National Judicial College, whose reading of the manuscript gave it the benefit of his expertise; David J. Langum, Cumberland School of Law; and James Hancock.

Colleagues at the University of Nevada, Reno, who provided work space were Susan Baker, Louis Marvick, and Robert E. Blesse; I am much in their debt. Richard L. Siegel's reflections on the capital punishment issue were useful. Marsha Urban and Michael Ashley did valuable service by installing computer programs.

Marvin R. Aaron, of Longview Community College, Lee's Summit, Missouri, was my guide and congenial traveling companion in Fort Smith, Arkansas. Juliet Galonska, Park Historian at the Fort Smith National Historic Site, freely gave me the benefit of her considerable knowledge of the Parker court; her colleague, Tom Wing, provided valuable assistance in the selection of illustrations.

Among the historians consulted, I am deeply appreciative of the information and insights of Larry D. Ball, Sr., of Arkansas State University, a leading authority on nineteenth-century law enforcement. Lawrence H. Larsen, of the University of Missouri, Kansas City, provided guidance on the nineteenth-century federal court system. Gordon Bakken, of California State University, Fullerton, gave the manuscript an authoritative reading. David Sundstrand had many astute observations on how to treat Parker as a figure of popular culture. Those who directed attention to sources that I otherwise would have overlooked include Christopher G. Driggs, Nevada State Archives; Addison S. Wilhite, Special Collections Department, University of Nevada, Reno; and John Phillip Reid, School of Law, New York University.

Librarians who gave unstintingly of their time and professional skill were those at the University of Nevada, Reno, especially those of the Business and Government Information Center; the Nevada State Library, Carson City; the University of Missouri, Kansas City; the Kansas Judicial Center, Topeka; and the National Judicial College, Reno.

Among the many persons who gave support, advice, information, and encouragement are Clara M. Rollen, National Archives and Records Administration, Central Plains Region; Kenneth L. Irby, University of Kansas; David L. Harvey; Curtis S. Gibson; Kenneth J. Peak, University of Nevada, Reno; William A. Dobak, National Archives and Records Administration; Bob L. Blackburn and Sharon Ashton, both of the Oklahoma Historical Society; Marlin Shipman, Arkansas State University; Maggie Eirenschmalz; Barbara Rust, National Archives and Records Administration, Southwest Region; Marene Sweeney, National Archives, Rocky Mountain Region; H. Franklin Waters, Senior Judge, United States District Court, Western District of Arkansas; and Howard F. Sachs, Senior Judge, United States District Court, Western District of Missouri. Richard W. Etulain, editor of The Oklahoma Western Biographies series, went over the manuscript carefully and supplied many corrections and useful suggestions. Jean Hurtado, acquisitions editor of the University of Oklahoma Press, was patient and helpful. Katrin Flechsig, of the School of Law, the University of Texas at Austin, did a thoroughly professional job as copyeditor. My wife Hwa-di was, as always, supportive throughout.

Introduction

ISAAC Charles Parker is among America's best-known judicial figures. Many people who are unable to name any of the members of the United States Supreme Court can readily identify the "Hanging Judge" of Fort Smith, Arkansas.

Parker's reputation rests on his tenure as judge of the United States District Court for the Western District of Arkansas, which lasted from his appointment by President Ulysses S. Grant in 1875 until his death in 1896. What distinguished this court from others in the federal judicial system was the unusually large number of criminal cases it heard and the many death sentences it handed down. This was because the district, in addition to embracing the counties of western Arkansas, had jurisdiction over the vast Indian Territory to the west. Throughout Parker's time and before, it was a notoriously lawless land. The judge never believed that the citizens of the Five Civilized Tribes who inhabited the territory were the main cause of the problem; rather, he placed most of the blame on white intruders and on the failure of the federal government to provide adequate protection for the legitimate residents. The deputy United States marshals employed by his court patrolled the area, arrested suspected lawbreakers, and hauled them to Fort Smith for trial before the much-feared judge. But neither Parker, the deputies and their posses, the Indian tribal police, nor the army were successful in curbing rampant criminality in the territory.

There are those who admire Parker because they see him as a tough law-and-order man who dealt out severe punishment to those who richly deserved it. Such people express the wish that there were more such judges—dispensers of stern justice who would neither coddle criminals nor be bothered by the niggling technicalities of the law. And then there are those who find him appalling, who see him as a cruel, arbitrary, remorseless instrument of society's vengeful impulses. Still others confuse him with Roy Bean, and picture him as a colorful ignoramus holding court behind a bar located somewhere west of the Pecos, with a pistol as a gavel.

All of these images, especially the last, miss the mark. Isaac C. Parker was a reasonably learned, dignified federal judge who came to the bench well suited by experience and temperament to perform the work required of him. The law made the death sentence mandatory for those whom the juries of his court found guilty of murder or rape. Admirers and detractors alike need to know that he took no delight in sending people to the gallows and that he was not unalterably committed to capital punishment. It will surprise many to learn that he sought executive clemency for several of those convicted in his court.

Parker usually has been seen as a law enforcement figure. But judges do not enforce the law; they *interpret* it. This study will focus, as any judicial biography should, on Parker as an interpreter of the law, examining his opinions and rulings in criminal, civil, and equity cases, habeas corpus proceedings, and instructions to grand and petit juries. Many of these are found in a hitherto little-used source for Parker's judicial prose, the first several volumes of the *Federal Reporter*; a few others are found in the *Federal Cases* series.

Only a small percentage of the trials over which Parker presided involved capital crimes, and less than half of the people he sentenced to death were executed. Most of his cases concerned liquor violations, timber poaching, and horse theft, as well as more serious offenses such as manslaughter and assault with intent to kill. Unlike other federal tribunals, his caseload involved few civil suits, but they too merit attention and receive it here.

For most of his time on the federal bench, there was no appeal to a higher court. When appeals to the United States Supreme Court were finally allowed, many of Parker's decisions were reversed, a situation that filled his last years with bitterness. His subsequent indecorous attacks on the Court and the Department of Justice have reflected negatively on his reputation.

Because Parker's judicial duties took up so much of his daily life, and because a tornado swept away most of his personal papers shortly after his death, biographies have tended to focus almost exclusively on his public life. This examination of his career is no exception. In fact, it is perhaps as much a study of his court as of the man. I have attempted to emphasize that Parker's tribunal was, despite its uniqueness in some important respects, part of the federal judiciary. Its judge was bound by the same precedents and laws as the other federal courts. Like the others, the Fort Smith court was under the supervision of the Department of Justice, and, after 1889, its rulings and verdicts were subject to review by the Supreme Court and the Circuit Court of Appeals. As were other federal jurists of that period, Parker was both a district and circuit court judge. Except for the large number of deputy marshals, his court's personnel did not markedly differ from other courts within the system.

Whatever the criticisms that might legitimately be leveled at him, Isaac C. Parker was a man of integrity, dedication to duty, and even compassion. In the eyes of many, he is America's greatest trial judge.

Isaac C. Parker

CHAPTER I

Young Man Going Places

THE ambitious country boy choosing the law as the way to make his mark had become an old and familiar story long before the end of the nineteenth century. Isaac Charles Parker exemplifies this phenomenon; he became and remains America's most famous trial judge.

The family of Isaac Parker's father, Joseph Parker, had been long-time inhabitants of western Maryland. Joseph moved to Jefferson County, Ohio, where he purchased two sections of land in 1815. Later he moved to Belton County, in southeastern Ohio, and married Jane Shannon, whose family had been in the state since 1794. Joseph Parker had the reputation of "a man of remarkable energy, strict in domestic discipline, but mild and persuasive in his methods." Isaac, the couple's youngest child, was born in a log cabin on October 15, 1838, near Barnesville, Ohio.

The educational opportunities open to him, although not great, were certainly an improvement over the primitive frontier schooling available to Abraham Lincoln, an Ohio Valley log-cabin boy of a generation earlier. Young Isaac received his primary education at Breeze Hill School. Next he attended a private academy, the Barnesville Classical Institute. To finance his studies there, he taught in a country school for four years.

Isaac Parker alternated school work with helping out on the family farm. Like Lincoln, young Isaac much preferred book-learning to farm work. According to family tradition, he read while resting from his duties in the hayfield. His reading tastes ran toward literature and even more toward history. Among his favorite books were Washington Irving's *Life of Washington*, George Bancroft's strongly nationalistic *History of the United States*, and Thomas McCauley's *History of England*. While at the Barnesville institute, Isaac Parker developed into an enthusiastic and tenacious debater.

A strict Methodist upbringing also did much to shape Parker's character and outlook. This was largely the work of his mother, "a woman remarkable for her strong mental qualities and business habits, possessing great force of character." Jane Parker made sure that Isaac became a deep and faithful student of the Bible. A profound religiosity was later to mark his judicial pronouncements. His belief in a stern but just and merciful God remained unshakable.

His mother's family, the Shannons, were the source of another important influence on his life. Six of her uncles were lawyers and men of affairs in Ohio and the nation. The most prominent was Wilson Shannon. A county prosecutor, twice governor of the state, minister to Mexico, congressman, and territorial governor of Kansas, Shannon was a major force in Democratic circles; he was no doubt an inspiration to his great-nephew. Becoming a lawyer was an obvious career choice for one seeking to follow in his illustrious relative's footsteps.

There were few law schools in the United States in the years of Parker's youth, and probably none within his financial and geographic reach. So at age seventeen he began preparing for his chosen profession in the same way most aspiring lawyers in America had since colonial days: he read the law. That is, he began clerking in the office of a local attorney. There he learned the proper way to draw up wills, contracts, and other routine legal documents; studied his employer's courtroom techniques; and availed himself of the volumes in his mentor's library. The standard authorities to be studied included *Greenleaf on Evidence*, Chancellor James Kent's *Commentaries on American Law*, Joseph Story's *Commentaries on Equity Jurisprudence*, and Sir William Blackstone's *Commentaries on the English Law*. "Such a system," biographer Roger Tuller has written, "produced gen-

erations of generalists, vague on the technicalities of the law
but gifted in swaying juries and judges through a combination of spell-binding oratory and acute logic."

Bar examinations of the period were usually informal, per-
functory, and undemanding. Isaac Parker passed his in 1859.
The next decision was where to launch his professional life.
He chose a city in what was then the West: Saint Joseph, in
Buchanan County, Missouri.

Influencing his choice was the presence in Saint Joseph of
one of his great-uncles, D. E. Shannon, who had recently set
up a law practice in the bustling Missouri River town. Then,
too, his great-uncle Wilson Shannon was across the river serving his term as governor of Kansas Territory. Also across the
Missouri was a neophyte lawyer named David J. Brewer, who
arrived in Leavenworth, Kansas the same year (1859) Isaac
Parker came to Saint Joseph. Brewer also would achieve prom-
inence as a jurist—in his case, as a justice of the United States
Supreme Court—and his path and Parker's would cross in
due time.

By 1860 Saint Joseph was a community of nearly 9,000
inhabitants. Among Missouri cities, it was second only to
Saint Louis in population and commercial importance. The
city census of that year enumerated 41 "free colored" and no
slaves; Buchanan County had 51 free colored and 2,011
slaves out of a total population of 23,861. In 1859, "Saint
Joe" became the western terminus of the Hannibal and St.
Joseph Railroad, the first railroad to cross Missouri. Saint
Joseph was a major river port and trade center and a popular
jumping-off place for the wagon trains of overland immi-
grants. It vied with Leavenworth and Atchison, Kansas, and
with other river communities in Missouri to become the
dominant city in the "elbow region" of the Missouri River.
Shortly, Kansas City, Missouri, would gain the prize, in part
because it secured its own rail connection with the Hannibal
and St. Joseph and it was the first to build a bridge across the
Missouri River. Nevertheless, Saint Joseph continued to be a

town of considerable importance and a good place for an up-and-coming young man to begin a law career. In 1860 young Isaac Parker was one of 1,187 lawyers in Missouri.

Not long after stepping off the steamboat, the 200-pound, six-foot, blue-eyed Parker began practicing in the Market Square offices of D. E. Shannon and H. B. Branch. The firm became "Branch, Shannon, and Parker." The partnership's business included casework in the counties of northwestern Missouri that constituted the Twelfth Judicial Circuit as well as in Kansas Territory and before the Missouri Supreme Court. Before the end of 1859 the partnership dissolved, and Parker continued alone in what was to be his brief career as an attorney in private practice.

Remaining in Market Square, in the center of Saint Joseph's commercial life, Parker enjoyed what was apparently modest success in a practice covering most branches of the law. He drew up wills and contracts, filed land claims, and argued on behalf of clients in the courtrooms of the circuit. Among those he represented were persons accused of crimes. For example, Circuit Judge Silas Woodson appointed Parker to defend John Dick, who was charged with the "felonious wounding" of another. The result was a conviction with a sentence of four years at hard labor. Civil practice also gave Parker problems. He had to sue at least two former clients who were unable or unwilling to pay him the fees he had earned on their behalf. From one of them he was awarded two horses, a wagon, and a harness.

Despite such headaches, young Parker's practice continued to grow. By 1861 his reputation was solid enough for him to consider seeking elective office, and he had met the residency requirement for doing so.

Parker was a Democrat and an adherent of the Stephen A. Douglas wing of the party. He had defended Senator Douglas's fateful handiwork, the Kansas-Nebraska Act. In 1854 Congress had passed the Illinois senator's bill organizing the new territories of Kansas and Nebraska. The act repealed the Missouri Compromise of 1821, which had prohibited the spread of slavery in the territories north of the latitude of 36°30'. Douglas's principle of "Popular Sovereignty" replaced the absolute prohibition of slavery by permitting the citizens of the territories to either adopt or reject the institution. At first, most northern and southern Democrats embraced what they believed to be a feasible solution to the vexing question of slavery in the territories. Many northern Democrats, however, did not, and several defected to the new Republican party, which opposed slavery in the territories. Before long, Isaac C. Parker would be among their number.

People assumed that Kansas Territory, situated next to the slave state of Missouri, would adopt slavery. The assumption proved disastrously wrong. Bloody confrontations between pro- and anti-slavery forces made Kansas a national issue, further splitting parties and sections. By the time Parker arrived in Missouri, the worst of the turmoil in the territory had subsided, and its governor, Parker's great-uncle Wilson Shannon, presided over relative calm.

Nevertheless, slavery and other issues continued to widen the gap between the northern and southern states, and civil war erupted in 1861. Contributing to the breakup of the Union was the splitting of the Democratic party into sectional wings in 1860. Douglas was the standard bearer of its northern wing in the presidential election of that year. During the campaign, Parker organized a local Stephen A. Douglas Club. Most of the slave states, unwilling to accept the election of Republican Abraham Lincoln, began the process of secession.

Hostilities broke out in April 1861. That month, Parker, still a Democrat, was elected Saint Joseph's city attorney. It was a part-time position, and the term was for one year. Nevertheless, the duties of the job were varied and the young man made the most of it. He was to represent Saint Joseph in all actions in which the city was a party, serve as advisor to the city council, prosecute violations of municipal ordinances before the justice of the peace and the county recorder, and bring appeals to higher courts. The pay was modest: $2.50 for each conviction in the municipal courts, $5.00 for winning an appeal. When not performing his official duties, he continued his private practice.

One of Parker's first tasks was to advise the city council regarding claims against workmen of a street crew whose negligence, it was contended, caused a building to collapse; eventually the council agreed to pay compensation. Other actions stemmed from deaths of horses caused allegedly by an open evacuation on a city street and from a "dangerous" embankment.

Appearing before the council on behalf of the city's police force, Parker argued successfully for a pay increase for the day shift of the police force. He was likewise effective in persuading the council to respond favorably to a citizens' petition complaining against enforcement of an ordinance that permitted the destruction of swine running free in the streets.

Given Parker's later reputation as the scourge of lawbreakers in the Indian Territory, it is not surprising to learn that as city attorney, he was a vigorous foe of crime in Saint Joseph. Certainly there was plenty of it. Saint Joseph was still a frontier town, with the usual complement of lawbreakers; being a river town and a border town exacerbated the situation. The miscreants Parker dealt with were, however, minor offenders. More serious malefactors were tried before the circuit court. Public intoxication accounted for the majority of his cases. He secured a conviction for drunkenness against the city's founder, Joseph Robideaux. Much of the remaining caseload was also drinking-related: assault, brawling, "obstreperous conduct," patronizing brothels, and offensive language.

The primary problems of maintaining law and order in northwestern Missouri at this time lay outside the city attorney's bailiwick. The Civil War, waged in Missouri, had especially frightening consequences for civilians as well as soldiers. Missouri, a slave state, remained nominally within the Union fold. Throughout the conflict, however, its people, including the citizenry of Buchanan County, remained sharply divided between the Union and Confederate loyalties. Missouri contributed fighting men to both sides, and much of the fighting

took place within its borders. There were major engagements, such as the Battle of Wilson's Creek. The situation in
the western part of the state was made more grim by the presence of vicious gangs of pro-Confederate and pro-Union
guerrillas. Missouri "Bushwhackers" and Kansas "Jayhawk-
ers" not only battled each other but committed atrocities on
the civilian populations of both states. Adding to the woes of
Missouri noncombatants were stringent measures aimed at
Confederate sympathizers. Union commanders such as John
C. Frémont and Thomas Ewing were especially detested for
imposing these restrictions.

In this atmosphere, neutrality was impossible. In the first
months of the secession crisis but before the outbreak of hostilities, Parker tried to convince his audience at a "Working-
men's Meeting" on February 8, 1861, that compromise was
still possible. Once it was apparent that compromise was not
possible, he emerged as a solid supporter of the Union.

In the midst of these ominous developments, Parker experienced a happy change in his private life—the end of bache-
lorhood. On December 12, 1861, he and Mary O'Toole
were united in matrimony. "Laughing, dark-eyed" Mary was
the daughter of an Irish immigrant father and a Missouri-
born mother. She had graduated from the Convent of the
Sacred Heart in Saint Joseph. The O'Tooles were apparently
as firm in their Catholicism as the Parkers were in their
Methodism, but any tensions resulting from religious difference did not prevent Isaac and Mary from having a successful
and loving marriage.

Unlike many other politically ambitious professional men,
Parker did not seek glory as a full-time participant in the war
that broke out in the spring of 1861. He did, however, serve
part-time in the military for much of the conflict. His earliest
service may have been with Company A of the 61st Missouri
Emergency Regiment. On July 30, 1862, at Saint Joseph, he
joined Company G of the 25th Regiment, Enrolled Missouri
Militia, and was ordered into active service August 7. The
next month he was detailed as a deputy provost marshal. He

was relieved from duty with the 25th Regiment on February 20, 1863, and the regiment was disbanded in November because, according to a county history, the militiamen of Buchanan County "had become demoralized." In 1864 another home guard regiment, the 87th, was organized. Parker was enrolled in Company G on April 30 of that year and was ordered into active service on June 3. In October he was "detailed to report to Col. [James W.] Strong," a duty that lasted into the following month. His active service apparently ended later that year. He received credit for 97 days of "actual" service, during which he attained the rank of corporal. Although Missouri was far from the major centers of the war, it was the scene of many battles and lesser engagements, and some sources say that Parker was involved in a few minor skirmishes. The *Congressional Directory* for 1872 even credits him with raising a company for the First Nebraska Infantry in 1861. Although Parker's military credentials are not impressive, they were sufficient to show his loyalty to the Union cause in a bitterly split community and state.

Intermittent soldiering permitted Parker to continue performing his duties as city attorney, but even in his civilian capacity, he felt the impact of the war. A local ordinance forbade the flying of flags that might inflame public passions. When a constable took down an American flag displayed in front of a private residence, Union sympathizers protested. The constable asked Parker for an interpretation of the ordinance. The city attorney found it applicable only to party banners.

Running on an "Unconditional Union Ticket," Parker was elected to a second term in 1862 and a third term in 1863. With mixed results, he sought reversal in the circuit court of judgments against the city, all involving small amounts, including his fees.

By 1864 he had taken his Union sympathies to their logical conclusion and had become a Republican. He was also ready to capitalize on his good reputation and seek higher office, namely the post of attorney for the Twelfth Circuit. Parker soon learned that "bolting" one's party was a serious matter in nineteenth-century America. Angry Democrats branded him a turncoat. While he was speaking at a rally on April 2, three Democrats menaced him with horsewhips. Parker faced them down, telling them they would "die considerably before [their] time" should they attempt to carry out their threat. He then announced that the Democratic mayor of Saint Joseph had threatened his life.

Parker not only won the race for circuit attorney but was also chosen as one of Missouri's electors in the 1864 presidential election, casting his ballot for the reelection of Abraham Lincoln. For the next few years, the Republican party enjoyed dominance in Missouri, and as a convert to its ranks, Parker benefitted accordingly.

Parker took over his new post on March 20, 1865. The circuit consisted of Buchanan County and six other counties. According to Missouri's General Statutes of that year, a circuit attorney's job was to "commence and prosecute all civil and criminal actions in which the state, or any county in his circuit may be concerned; defend all suits brought against the state, or any county of his circuit; prosecute forfeited recognizances and actions for the recovery of debts, fines, penalties and forfeitures accruing to the state, or any county in his circuit." He was to give his opinion, when required and without fee, to justices of the peace and county courts on points of law in criminal cases and in cases in which the state or a county was involved.

In addition to arguing civil cases on behalf of the state and counties, Parker prosecuted more serious categories of crimes than he had as a city attorney. It was now his job to see to it that thieves, burglars, arsonists, and murderers were convicted. On his first day he prosecuted twenty-five defendants, and by the end of the March session, 161 actions. Not all were charged with serious offenses; the majority of those hauled before the bar stood accused of such infractions as selling liquor without a license, gambling, and running bawdy houses. Even the robbery and larceny cases tended to be petty affairs.

Because Parker's pay was only four hundred dollars a year, he continued private practice. In 1865 Parker, his wife's brother-in-law Jefferson Chandler, and an attorney named Strong formed a partnership. Inevitably, there were conflicts between Parker's public and private practices. For instance, he had to withdraw as prosecutor in an arson case because his law firm was representing the accused.

Parker's income became for him sufficient to purchase a house in a desirable neighborhood, on the corner of Thirteenth and Felix streets. By 1870 the Parker household, in addition to Isaac and Mary, consisted of twenty-seven-year-old Thomas (perhaps Parker's brother-in-law Thomas B. Burnet, listed on the census as an Ohio-born lawyer) and two black servants: nineteen-year-old Etta (or perhaps Elsa?) Mason and twelve-year-old Alice Mason.

No doubt Parker was skilled as an attorney and did well in private practice, but he continued to seek public office. He resigned as circuit attorney in 1867 to seek the judgeship of the Twelfth Circuit in 1868. He defeated his Democratic opponent handily, by 1,301 to 922 votes. The term was for six years. The salary, paid by the state, was two thousand dollars per year. The law required each county to contribute to the circuit judge an additional two hundred dollars per year.

Missouri's twenty-two circuit courts were grouped within six judicial districts. Parker's tribunal was within the Fifth District. The district courts heard appeals from the circuit courts, and decisions of the district courts could be appealed to the state supreme court. The circuit judges served as the judges of the district courts.

The circuit courts had plenary jurisdiction that extended to "all criminal cases which shall not be otherwise provided by law," and had "exclusive original jurisdiction in all civil cases which shall not be cognizable before the county courts and justices of the peace, and not otherwise provided by law." These courts also had concurrent original jurisdiction with the justices of the peace in cases arising from contracts in which the debt, balance due, or damages claimed were more than fifty dollars and not more than ninety dollars, and in all actions for injuries to persons or property wherein the damages claimed were more than twenty dollars and not more than fifty dollars. Circuit courts had appellate jurisdiction in cases heard originally in the county and justice courts, over which courts the circuit judge had "a superintending control." Finally, circuit courts had "a general control over executors, administrators, guardians, curators, minors, idiots, lunatics, and persons of unsound mind." The judge was to hold two terms a year in each of the counties, except Buchanan, which had four terms.

Throughout his career as a jurist, Parker, like most other American practitioners of the law in the latter half of the nineteenth century, adhered to legal formalism. This form of jurisprudence called for close following of precedent and the precepts of legal authorities such as Britain's Sir William Blackstone and America's James Kent.

Brief though Parker's career as a Missouri jurist was, he gained valuable experience that prepared him for greater judicial responsibility in the future. He also established patterns of hard work and kept up with a crowded docket. After taking his place on the bench in January 1869, the new judge set about his tasks with alacrity. As did other circuit courts of the state, Parker's conducted business six days a week. Establishing practices that would serve him well in his career as a judge of a busy federal court, he expedited matters by encouraging guilty pleas and quick dismissals. Witnesses who failed to appear were treated to swift and certain punishment, which sometimes meant attachment of their property. For bail-jumping defendants he issued warrants. The judge and his court were not to be trifled with. Yet the judge was not remarkably more severe in his sentencing than those who preceded him as judges of the Twelfth Circuit. For example, he sentenced a man to seven years for grand larceny and another to a three-month jail term and a fine of a hundred dollars for assault with intent to kill. Considering Parker's later reputation, it is worth noting that he handed down no death sentences during his tenure as a state judge. Had he served longer in this capacity, perhaps opportunities to do so would have presented themselves. Before they did, he chose to end his Missouri judicial career in favor of a run at a seat in the United States House of Representatives.

Buchanan County was within the state's Seventh Congressional District. The Republican incumbent, Representative Joel F. Asper, was favored to retain his seat in the 1870 election. By that time, however, Missouri Republicanism was split into two irreconcilable factions. The Radical Republicans stood by the provision of the state's self-reconstructing constitution of 1865, which disfranchised those supporters of the late Confederacy who refused to swear an oath of loyalty to the nation. The Liberal Republicans advocated a relaxation of the provision. The two wings differed also in their stands on the tariff, the Radicals supporting high, protective duties and the Liberals favoring lower rates. Unable to settle their differences at the state convention, the two wings ran as separate parties.

In the Seventh Congressional District, Parker emerged as the choice of the Radical Republicans. He and his followers squared off against the incumbent Asper at the district convention in September of 1870. Fortunately for Parker, his adherents were in positions to secure his victory. Chairing the committee on credentials was Jefferson Chandler, Parker's law partner, who saw to it that several pro-Parker delegates were seated, despite dubious credentials. The chairman of the convention, also a Parker man, denied seats to seven black would-be delegates who were committed to Asper. Finally, in an unexplained move, Buchanan County's Asper delegates swung to Parker on the first ballot. The vote was eighty-four to eighty-three for Parker; the convention then declared the nomination unanimous.

Thrust before the convention by his elated supporters, the nominee thanked them for the honor and expressed his gratitude to the "mechanics, laborers and artisans" who had launched his public career in Saint Joseph, Buchanan County.

He pledged his support of the state Radical ticket and its platform, including the hard line on test oaths. To dedicate all of
his energies to the campaign, as well as to preserve the dignity of the judiciary, he announced that he would resign his
judgeship.

The Liberal opposition was, of course, outraged at Parker's
victory. Through the pages of their organ, the *Saint Joseph
Herald*, they cried fraud, denouncing Jefferson Chandler's
actions and accusing him of bribery. In their eyes Parker was
a "chronic bolter." The Liberals prevailed upon Asper to
oppose the Radical nominee in the general election.

In the unpleasant campaign that followed, the Liberals cast
doubt on Parker's loyalty to the Union at the start of the Civil
War. He lashed back with the accusation that Asper's backers
were the real bolters. More recklessly, Parker charged that
Buchanan County Republicans were "hopelessly depraved"
and branded Saint Joseph a "hell-hole." When not engaged
in such vituperation, he spoke out for the reelection of
Radical Joseph W. McClurg for governor, for a high tariff,
and for the continued disfranchisement of unrepentant seces-
sionists.

Parker's chances improved when Asper announced his
withdrawal from the contest. The Liberals replaced him with
another candidate. Parker was victorious in the November
balloting, but by a narrower margin than he had predicted.
Elsewhere in Missouri the Radical candidates, including
McClurg, fared less well.

At the close of 1870, Congressman-elect Isaac C. Parker,
then thirty-two years old, could look back on more than a
decade of success in the legal profession and rapid political
advancement. He had shown himself to be ambitious, aggres-
sive, and, considering his shifting political loyalties, something of an opportunist. Such qualities were not detriments
to the rise of a young man, particularly in the rough-and-
tumble political life of postwar Missouri. His political skills
and his record in the 42d Congress were strong enough to
get him elected to a second term in 1874.

Hitherto Parker had served as an interpreter and upholder of the law. After taking his seat in the House of Representatives on March 4, 1871, he immersed himself in the processes of making law. His assignments to the House's standing committees included the Committee on the Territories and the Committee on Naval Appropriations and Expenditures.

Like the majority of congressmen, Parker introduced most of his legislation with his constituents in mind. As with the great majority of bills introduced by members of Congress, especially freshman members, most of his proposed legislation was tabled, died in committee, or was killed in the Senate. For example, he labored mightily but unsuccessfully for the erection of a new federal building for Saint Joseph. Other bills of interest to the voters of his district were for the construction of bridges over the Missouri River at Saint Joseph and Booneville and the granting of swamplands "for school purposes" to Holt County, which was within his district. Another measure he proposed was for paying three hundred dollars to T. H. Logan and D. T. McCoy to cover expenses and as a reward for capturing an escaped convict. He also sought to expand the jurisdiction of the United States District Court for the Western District of Missouri and to hold terms of the court in Saint Joseph and Springfield in addition to the terms held in Kansas City.

Among the many petitions sent to Parker by citizens of the Seventh Congressional District that he presented to the House were those urging the repeal of the federal duties on tobacco and licorice; another petition sought relief for the Southern Methodist Publishing House. He succeeded in persuading his colleagues to send a letter to the secretary of war, requesting that the secretary inform the House whether the present occupants of Hot Springs, Arkansas, or the United States held title to the mineral springs there.

In addition to pushing bills for the benefit of the Seventh District, Parker was able to get several private pension bills enacted. Northern Republican congressmen of the later nineteenth century were especially zealous in seeking to reward "worthy" Union veterans or their widows not covered by the general pension laws. Not all of the beneficiaries were truly deserving, but it was good politics for lawmakers to get this sort of federal largesse into the statute books.

In matters relating to Reconstruction, the freshman representative stayed true to the Radical cause with his votes and rhetoric. Parker consistently voted for legislation to enforce the Thirteenth, Fourteenth, and Fifteenth Amendments to the Constitution. For example, he voted for civil rights measures and against an attempt to weaken the Ku Klux Klan Act of 1871. On the other hand, he introduced two bills to relieve four men from "the political disabilities imposed upon them by the fourteenth amendment to the Constitution of the United States." Parker also pushed a proposal to provide benefits for Missouri's Unionist militia and to the survivors of Union troops killed by "Bloody Bill" Anderson's rebel guerrillas at Centralia, Missouri. This bill became one of the few by Parker signed into law. When Representative James G. Blair, a Missouri Liberal Republican, spoke out for a general amnesty for all former supporters of the Confederacy, Parker responded with denunciations of the "treason" of the slave power and its minions. All citizens, he said, "should not only cease to justify the rebellion, but should commence to denounce it as a crime, and not only as a crime of ordinary extent, but one that was extremely wicked."

On these and other issues Parker proved himself a staunch supporter of the policies of President Ulysses S. Grant and his wing of the Republican party, the "Stalwarts." Yet he was not content to confine his interests to constituency and party concerns. In addition, he proposed an amendment to the Constitution that would prohibit members of Congress from seeking the presidency of the United States during their terms and for two years after. The proposal died in committee, as did a somewhat more surprising measure he advanced that would have given the vote to women in the territories. This was not entirely without precedent, for Wyoming and Utah territories had already extended the franchise to females.

Parker's most important committee service was as a member of the House Committee on the Territories. In this he was following in the footsteps of his first political idol, Stephen A. Douglas, who had served conspicuously in the committees on territories in both the House and the Senate. The duties of the committee's nine members were "to examine into the legislative, civil, and criminal proceedings of the Territories, and to devise and report to the House such means as, in their opinion, may be necessary to secure the rights and privileges of residents and non-residents."

As a representative from Missouri, one of the westernmost American states, Parker's assignment to the committee was a logical one. He focused his attention on one territory in particular: Indian Territory. Occupying much of present-day Oklahoma, it was not a territory in the traditional sense. Ordinarily, a territory had a governor and other federally appointed officials, a legislature chosen by the voters, and elective local officials. Territorial status was intended to prepare its people for eventual statehood and a greater measure of self-government. But Indian Territory was another matter. It was a collection of five completely separate "nations," each occupied by one of the "Five Civilized Tribes," the Creeks, Cherokees, Seminoles, Chickasaws, and Choctaws. Although some came to the territory voluntarily, most tribal members had been driven from their homelands in the southeastern United States and compelled to resettle in an area that many assumed would be a permanent home, free from white intrusion, and with little likelihood of becoming a state. While each of the nations was to a large extent self-governing, the United States retained sovereignty over them.

During the Civil War, elements of all five tribes sided with the Confederacy, and as punishment, the federal government reduced the boundaries of the nations. In the last decades of the nineteenth century, the federal government relocated several Kansas and Nebraska tribes, assigning them lands in the northeastern corner of the Cherokee Nation and further west in what was known as the Cherokee Outlet.

In many respects, the people of the Five Nations lived in much the same way as white westerners. They had elective administrative officers and legislative bodies, court systems, and town and county governments. Most of the Indian inhabitants were farmers or ranchers. There were churches, schools, retail stores, newspapers, and other trappings of civilization. Soon after the Civil War, railroads began to penetrate the Indian Territory, and whites, many of them illegally, started what became a flood of immigration.

At this point in his life, Parker, like most Americans of his generation, believed that the American Indians, including the "civilized" ones, were soon to disappear, the victims of encroaching white civilization. The problem then was to find humane yet practical solutions for the plight of the "dying race." Some Indian-hating westerners favored outright extermination, but the majority of concerned whites were divided between those who advocated assimilation into the dominant culture and those who believed the Indians were best served by setting them aside and protecting them from further incursion into their land and assaults on their culture. The Indians themselves were similarly in disagreement, split between traditionalists who resisted assimilation and "progressives" who embraced the idea.

Representative Parker shared the belief that assimilation was the best answer. Accordingly, on February 5, 1872, he introduced a bill with the heading "For the Better Protection of Indian Tribes and Their Consolidation Under a Civil Government to be Called the Territory of Oklahoma." It called for the reorganization of the Indian Territory along traditional lines: a governor, judges, and other territorial officers, all federally appointed, with the lawmaking power vested in an elective legislature. Parker maintained that this legislation would hasten the "civilizing" of the territory's inhabitants by having them participate in the white man's governing processes. At least initially, the legislators and other elected officials would be Indians. This, he argued, would enable the citizens of the territory to better protect their lands and

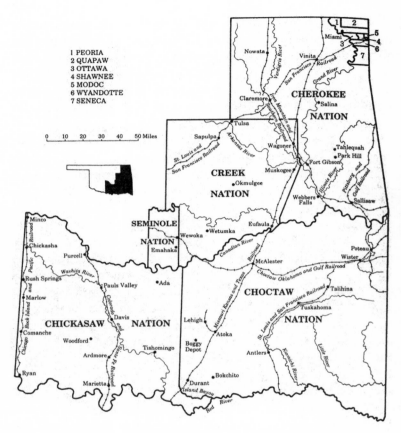

The Five Nations of Indian Territory and the Quapaw Agency, 1889. Reproduced from Jeffrey Burton, *Indian Territory and the United States, 1866–1906: Courts, Government, and the Movement for Oklahoma Statehood* (Norman: University of Oklahoma Press, 1995, 150).

rights. Following considerable debate, the bill was tabled; when Parker presented the proposal again nearly a year later, it died in committee. A third attempt got the bill to the floor of the House, where it was voted down. With the same lack of success, he reintroduced a similar measure in his second term.

Those opposed to the bill argued that treaties between the tribes and the federal government in 1866 made the status of the Five Nations inviolable. Parker responded that Congress had the "inherent right . . . to exercise [its] sovereign power whenever the Representatives of the people believe it ought to be exercised in the interests of humanity, in behalf of justice, and to give security to the property and lives of this people of this nation."

Spokesmen for the Creek and Cherokee tribes protested the attempts by Parker and others to create an Oklahoma Territory. In reply to Parker's remark that the Committee on the Territories saw no real conflict between his Oklahoma bill and the treaties of 1866, they professed to be "amazed at such a statement, for there is scarcely one of these treaties it does not break, or the spirit of which it does not violate."

Parker's bill was nothing new. Similar measures were regularly advanced throughout the second half of the nineteenth century. Their supporters might have been interested in the future well-being of the Indians, but surely they realized that any such reorganization of the Indian Territory would lay it open to white settlement and the inevitable destruction of the Indian ways of life. Opponents of the proposals were quick to point out this problem. They also charged that the end of Indian autonomy would allow railroad corporations to acquire large land grants carved out of formerly Indian lands. Delegates from the Five Nations joined congressional opponents in denouncing Parker's bills. In time, using the same arguments, Parker would himself speak out against attempts to change the form of the Indian Territory government and to open it up to unrestricted white settlement.

Another of Parker's proposals was to allow Indians "in certain cases" to acquire lands under the terms of the Homestead Act. The House adopted a resolution he introduced that called for the issuing and delivery of bonds to the Choctaw and Chickasaw nations, as agreed to in treaties between the United States and the two tribes.

Among the other Parker bills relating to the Indian Territory was one for the construction of a wagon road over the Red River in the Choctaw Nation. He also supported measures for the incorporating of western railroads, some of which would run through the lands of the Five Nations.

In 1872, Parker sought and gained reelection to the United States House of Representatives. As a member of the 43d Congress, his sole committee assignment was to the Committee on Appropriations. Membership in this important body indicates the esteem in which he was held by the House leadership. In his second term he introduced the usual bills for payments of claims and pensions to his constituents. The most notable speech of his second term was in support of the proposed budget for the Bureau of Indian Affairs. His remarks included impassioned rhetoric on the wrongs that the United States had inflicted on the Indians, which he said justified more funds to feed and otherwise care for them.

The elections of 1874 ended Parker's relatively brief but noteworthy congressional career. By then the majority of voters in Missouri's Seventh District had swung to the Democratic party. So too had most of the rest of the state's electorate. Rather than seek a third term and face certain defeat, Parker allowed himself to be the Republicans' sacrificial lamb in the choosing of a United States senator. Before the adoption of the Sixteenth Amendment of the Constitution (1917), state legislators chose the members of the United States Senate. Given the Democratic majority of the Missouri legislature, his candidacy was pro forma, and his defeat a foregone conclusion. When the legislature met in early 1875, it chose former Confederate brigadier general Francis M. Cockrell. Although Parker was never again to

serve in the national legislature, his congressional years provided him with contacts in Washington that would be helpful, in his later judicial career, for getting money and man-
power for his court.

A return to Saint Joseph and the private practice of law
apparently held no appeal for Parker. He was accustomed to
public office, and private practice could not match a seat in
Congress for personal gratification or political advancement.
So he looked to a source of employment familiar to out-of-
work politicians: federal patronage. As a Stalwart Republican,
he was politically deserving, and an offer from President
Grant was soon forthcoming: the chief justiceship of Utah
Territory. On March 16, 1875, the president sent Parker's
name to the United States Senate, which that day referred the
nomination to the Committee on the Judiciary, with all likelihood of a positive recommendation.

Parker, however, had second thoughts. Technically, the
tenure of a territorial justice could last until statehood. In
actuality it seldom did. The citizens of the territories saw the
justices as carpetbaggers and routinely made life miserable for
these outsiders. An appointment to the Utah bench was especially fraught with difficulties. There the Mormon majority
had long resented what they saw as prejudiced federal officials
bent upon assaulting their beliefs and way of life. Governors,
judges, and other Washington-appointed officials came and
went with great frequency. It was intended that Parker replace
Chief Justice James B. McKean, whose clashes with the
Mormon hierarchy had led to his removal in 1875.

Learning of another judicial post with far greater job security and fewer problems, Parker asked that the Utah nomination be withdrawn and that he be appointed to a vacancy in
the regular federal court system: the judgeship of the United
States District Court for the Western District of Arkansas, at
Fort Smith. The appointment at Fort Smith would not only
guarantee a permanent position, but also spare him, presumably, from the political pressures and hostile constituencies
that plagued the lives of territorial judges. Yet it is possible

that Parker did not originally intend to retain the Arkansas post for life. According to a deathbed statement, he and President Grant had agreed that Parker would hold the job only long enough to straighten out the chaotic affairs of the court. In any case, President Grant acceded to the Missourian's request, informing the Senate, on March 18, 1875, that he was withdrawing Parker's Utah nomination, as well as that of his original nominee for the Arkansas judgeship, Joseph Bonham Kinsman—nominating Parker instead. The upper house voted unanimously for confirmation.

As was true of all federal judgeships, the position was for life, or more correctly, "during good behavior." Only death, resignation, or removal through impeachment ended the tenure of a federal jurist. The adequate but not handsome annual compensation was three thousand, five hundred dollars.

Isaac C. Parker would soon begin presiding over one of the federal judiciary's more isolated tribunals, which was to become the nation's most notorious.

CHAPTER 2

A Town, a Court, and a Territory

ISAAC C. Parker arrived at Fort Smith, Arkansas, on the steamboat *Ella Hughes* on May 4, 1875. With him was his brother-in-law, attorney Thomas B. Burnett. He rode by carriage through a crowd of curious onlookers to his temporary quarters in the Le Flore Hotel. Mary and their son Charles C., born while Parker was serving his first term in Congress, joined him later.

Their new home was a town of about 2,500 people, located at the confluence of the Arkansas and Poteau rivers in northwestern Arkansas. By the end of the decade, the population would grow to more than 3,000. Fort Smith was the principal town of Sebastian County, which, according to the census of 1870, numbered 12,940 people, including 1,354 blacks and more than 40 Indians. When the Parkers settled there, Fort Smith lacked paved and lighted streets, sidewalks, decent hotels, and adequate public schools.

The community had evolved out of a settlement adjoining the military post of Fort Smith, which was established in 1817 and named for Brigadier General Thomas A. Smith. The original purpose of the post was to end conflict between Cherokee and Osage Indians and to facilitate westward migration. Soon, a major duty of the soldiers became the suppression of the illegal importation of liquor into nearby Indian Territory—an activity that would also become a major part of Judge Parker's docket.

In the pre-Civil War period, the army twice abandoned and twice relocated Fort Smith. At the outbreak of the war, Confederate forces took over the fort, controlling it and the

Isaac C. Parker around the time he assumed his duties as judge of the United States District Court for the Western District of Arkansas. *Fort Smith National Historic Site.*

surrounding area until 1863, when federal troops regained possession. An 1871 act of Congress provided for the transfer of the Fort Smith military reservation to the Department of the Interior, which was to dispose of the property. The last troops marched out later that year. Over the next several years, the government deeded or sold parts of the reservation, and the federal government transferred the remaining acreage to the city of Fort Smith.

Fort Smith, Arkansas, was smaller than Saint Joseph, Missouri, but in many respects the towns were similar. Like Saint Joseph at the time of Parker's 1859 settling there in 1859, Fort Smith was a busy river town and was becoming a railroad and manufacturing center. The Little Rock and Fort Smith line was the first to reach Fort Smith, arriving in 1876. A branch line of the St. Louis and San Francisco (known as the "Frisco") came to Fort Smith in 1882. That year the Frisco was granted a right of way through the Indian Territory; meanwhile trains were ferried across the Arkansas River between Fort Smith and Van Buren on barges. The Kansas and Arkansas Valley line cut through the Indian Territory and eventually extended from Fort Smith to Arkansas City, Kansas. Railroad magnate Jay Gould's Missouri Pacific Railway Company acquired the Little Rock and Fort Smith, and Gould suggested that the city construct a bridge across the Arkansas River. In 1888, a citizens' committee voted to give Missouri Pacific $25,000, with the understanding that the railroad would build a bridge across the river. The bridge opened in 1891, providing an important connection between northwestern Arkansas and the Indian Territory. In 1889 the St. Louis, Iron Mountain and Southern line linked Fort Smith with Greenwood, Arkansas. A branch line of the Kansas City Southern came to Fort Smith from Spiro, Indian Territory, in 1896.

Fort Smith was also a border town with its share of disreputable inhabitants and shady businesses. Still, like Saint Joseph, it became a stable community of some importance within the state. The facilities it lacked when Parker arrived

materialized soon thereafter. Fort Smith also attracted indus-
try—among the more important manufacturing concerns
that located there in the late nineteenth century were a plant
to compress cotton and produce cottonseed oil, facilities for
milling and storing grain, furniture manufacturing companies, and an ironworks.

A second son, James J., was born to Isaac and Mary Parker
a few years after their arrival in Fort Smith. By 1880 their
household consisted of the four Parkers and a German-born
domestic and seamstress, Lena Shulte. The Parker family soon
became leading and respected citizens of their community.

As a Republican, a former Union militiaman, and an out-
sider assuming office in a state of the late Confederacy, Parker
might be seen as a carpetbagger, but in most respects he was
not. Reconstruction in Arkansas ended soon after the state
elections of 1874, when the Democratic party won control of
the Arkansas government. As a Republican from outside the
state, Parker's advantage was not being associated with the
violent factional strife, the "Brooks-Baxter war", that had
recently torn Arkansas Republicanism apart. In fact, Arkansas's Republican senators, Powell Clayton and Stephen W.
Dorsey, had suggested to President Grant that he appoint
someone from out of state to the Western District bench.
Also, the immediate political environment was initially not as
unfriendly to Parker as one might suppose. There had been
strong pro-Union sentiment in northwestern Arkansas during
the Civil War, and an appreciable minority of the area's citizens continued to support the Republican party for several
years thereafter. Nevertheless, the 1874 election put a Democrat, Augustus H. Garland, in the governor's chair and gave
the legislature a Democratic majority. From then on, the for-
tunes of the Arkansas Republican party steadily declined.

The court over which Parker would preside for the next
twenty-one years was part of an illogical federal judicial structure. The Judiciary Act of 1789 created a three-tiered system
consisting of district courts, circuit courts, and the United
States Supreme Court. Congress determined which type of

cases were to be heard in what courts. Each state had at least one district court, each with a corresponding circuit court above it. The district judge sat on both courts. District courts had original jurisdiction only; circuit courts had original jurisdiction and a limited area of appellate jurisdiction.

At first the role of circuit judge was filled by the district judges and the Supreme Court justices, each of the latter assigned to a circuit consisting of several states. To relieve the justices of most of the burden of circuit court duty, Congress, in 1869, provided a judge for each of the nine circuits of the federal court system. The United States Courts for the Western and Eastern Districts of Arkansas were part of the Eighth Circuit, along with the federal courts of Minnesota, Iowa, Nebraska, Missouri, and Kansas. Later, Colorado, North and South Dakota, Wyoming, and Utah were added to the circuit when they were admitted to statehood. Because of the difficulty of covering the large area of the circuits, the new circuit judges were able to sit only sporadically with their district court brethren on the circuit courts. A district judge, in his capacity as a circuit judge, usually sat alone. Four men served as judge of the Eighth Circuit during Parker's time on the Fort Smith bench: John F. Dillon, who went on to fame as a treatise writer; George W. McCrary; David J. Brewer, who later served on the Supreme Court; and Henry C. Caldwell. The act of 1869 still required Supreme Court justices to ride their circuits once every two years.

The primary function of the courts of the United States was to adjudicate cases arising out of federal laws, treaties, and the Constitution. Congress greatly expanded the jurisdiction of the circuit courts in such cases by an act of 1875, the year that Parker was appointed to the federal bench. A circuit court's business involved cases of "diversity of citizenship," that is, civil cases in which the parties were from different states. The circuit courts thus provided a more neutral ground than the courts of the states of which the litigants were citizens, and the suits did not need to involve a federal question.

In the earliest years of the federal judiciary, the secretary of state oversaw the system of United States courts; later, Congress gave the responsibility to the secretary of the interior. With the creation of the Department of Justice in 1871 the attorney general took over the administration of the nation's tribunals.

As a component of this awkward system, the United States District Court for the Western District of Arkansas was itself an anomaly because most of the court's cases came not from Arkansas but from Indian Territory. Also, unlike other federal courts, most of the cases heard at Fort Smith were criminal rather than civil. When Arkansas was admitted to statehood in 1836, Congress created a United States District Court, seated at Little Rock. A major part of the Arkansas court's caseload was the adjudicating of matters arising out of the Intercourse Act of 1834, "An Act to regulate trade and intercourse with the Indian tribes and to preserve the peace on the frontiers." The main purpose of the 1834 act was to protect Indians from white intruders, such as whiskey peddlers, unauthorized hunters, coal thieves, and timber poachers. It provided for the federal trial of cases coming out of the Indian country in which at least one of the parties was white; for example, a white person accused of killing, assaulting, or robbing an Indian, or an Indian charged with a crime against a white person. After 1836, the federal tribunal closest to Indian Territory was in Arkansas. Thus, federal judges there heard not only the usual civil and criminal cases in Arkansas involving federal law, but also a multitude of criminal cases from the vast territory to the west.

In adjacent Indian Territory, the tribal courts of the Creek, Cherokee, Seminole, Chickasaw, and Choctaw nations tried cases in which Indians were the only parties. Indian Territory jurisdiction, however, was more complicated than it appears, because determining Indian citizenship was often a knotty problem. A white marrying an Indian was theoretically entitled to tribal citizenship, but the status of such persons was often in doubt. Complicating the situation even more was the presence of many black people in the territory, most of them former slaves of Indians. These freedmen and their descendants were also citizens of the various tribes, but their status was frequently questionable.

In addition to court systems, each of the Indian nations had its own law enforcement officials. The tribal courts had marshals, and there were locally elected sheriffs and constables. Mounted "lighthorse police," who had broader jurisdiction and more extensive powers than the sheriffs and constables, patrolled the nations in search of lawbreakers. Beginning in 1878, the federally operated Indian agencies in the territory also maintained police forces; some of their members held commissions as deputy United States marshals. The agency police, army, and deputy marshals had power over whites that the tribal authorities lacked.

Close observers of affairs in the Indian Territory insisted that the great majority of Indians there were law-abiding and that the large and growing number of whites was the source of most of the criminality. Isaac Parker became firmly convinced of this point of view. Toward the end of his life, he told a reporter: "The Indian Race is not one of criminals. There have been sporadic cases of crime among them it is true, but as a people they are good citizens." In 1895 he told a congressional committee that the white intruders were largely responsible for lawlessness in the Indian Territory. He believed that most instances of Indian crime resulted from contact with the vicious white element infesting the territory.

As a congressman, Parker had favored a traditional territorial government and eventual statehood for the Indian Territory. Not long after assuming his judicial duties, he reversed his views. Speaking of the Cherokee system of government, he told a congressional committee that replacing tribal self-government with territorial government and allowing whites to move freely into the Cherokee domain "would have precisely the same effect as our action toward the California Indian[;] . . . it would send them out as beggars without a dollar." He warned that unscrupulous men would "rush in there and persuade [the Indians] that they needed money to build a house or improve their lands, and in six months, if left with the ownership of the soil, they would not have a place to lay their heads in the country." Indians, he asserted, "protect their own people, so that there is not a pauper Indian in the whole Five Civilized Tribes." In Parker's view, territorial status would be "absolute cruelty."

In the latter part of the nineteenth century, the racial composition of Indian Territory changed dramatically. In 1870, the population of the Indian Territory was 68,152, of whom 59,367 or 87 percent were Indians. The remainder consisted of 6,378 blacks and 2,407 whites. By 1885, about 25,000 whites lived in the territory. The 1890 census of the Indian Territory (which did not include the new territory of Oklahoma) showed a total population of 178,097, of which only 51,336, or 28 percent, were Indians. The remainder were 109,393 whites (including those claiming Indian citizenship) and 18,636 blacks (including those claiming Indian citizenship).

The spread of the rail network greatly facilitated white migration. Even before Parker's arrival in Fort Smith in 1875, railroads began entering the lands of the Five Nations. By 1889 several had laid track in the territory: the Atchison, Topeka and Santa Fe; Gulf, Colorado and Santa Fe; Missouri, Kansas and Texas; and Southern Kansas. The coming of the railroads brought even greater problems of law enforcement. As Ed Bearss and Arrell M. Gibson tell us in their history of Fort Smith, "Each railhead and construction camp became a kind of Satan's paradise. These migrant communities included, in addition to the rough-and-ready, brawling construction crews, a wide assortment of tinhorn gamblers, thieves, prostitutes, whisky sellers, and other hoodlums."

Before Parker took his place on the Fort Smith bench, the United States District Court for the Western District of Arkansas had a troubled history. When Arkansas had but one district court, its Indian Territory jurisdiction proved difficult to exercise. Federal marshals and their deputies had to travel from Little Rock to apprehend and bring back Indian

Territory suspects. Their fees and expenses were costly burdens on a chronically underfunded court. Frequently, the federal lawmen requested assistance from Indian authorities, but such help was not always forthcoming.

Before 1878 the regular army often served as *posse comitatus* in the western territories. That year Congress attempted to curtail the use of army troops as lawmen except to protect Indians, police public lands, and enforce international neutrality laws. But a War Department general order, also in 1878, gave field commanders wide discretion to employ their soldiers in emergencies. In Parker's time the army continued to patrol eastern Indian Territory and to haul various miscreants to Fort Smith for trial: whiskey peddlers, illegal hunters, timber poachers, unlicensed livestock grazers, horse thieves, and unauthorized settlers. Nevertheless, the soldiers there were too few and too spread out to be a consistently effective constabulary.

Getting litigants and witnesses to make the long journey from Indian Territory to Little Rock was another problem. Witnesses were especially reluctant to testify when confronted with the prospect of long delays in the payment of their fees. Sometimes payment was in the form of vouchers worth only a fraction of their face value, and other times there was no payment at all. The situation improved with the advent of Isaac Parker, but, largely because of insufficient congressional appropriations, the new judge's efforts to assure prompt and full payment to witnesses and jurors were never completely successful.

Because of the Indian Territory's reputation for lawlessness, the people of Arkansas began demanding more effective mechanisms for suppressing crime in an area all too close to them. They saw the court at Little Rock as unable or unwilling to impose law and order. Many also believed that the territory's Indian courts were inadequate and unfair to whites. They steadfastly opposed proposals for a federal court within the Indian Territory; the notion of trials of whites before Indian juries was unthinkable.

Arkansans believed that the solution was to have two federal district courts in their state, the current one at Little Rock and a new one to be located on the western border. The new district would put federal justice closer to the Indian Territory and its disorder. An Arkansas court also meant all-white juries for trials of the territory's Indian, black, and white malefactors.

In 1846, Senator Chester Ashley of Arkansas introduced a bill to divide his state into two judicial districts, with the new court for the Western District to sit at Van Buren, on the border with the Indian Territory. The Van Buren court would have its own district attorney, marshal, clerk, and commissioners—but not its own judge. To save money, Ashley and others wanted to have a single judge for both the Eastern and Western Districts. Most Arkansans supported the measure, which was at first well received in Congress. The coming of the Mexican War, however, along with Ashley's death in 1848 and opposition from the powerful Democratic machine in Arkansas, delayed passage until 1851.

In its final form, which was signed into law by President Millard Fillmore, the statute was close to Ashley's original bill. The Western District consisted of nine counties in northwestern Arkansas. The Indian Territory was appended to, but not part of, the district. The judge, who was also the judge of the Eastern District, would hold two sessions annually in Van Buren. The offices of district attorney and marshal were presidential appointments; the judge selected the clerk and commissioners. The law did not provide for a separate circuit court, but granted circuit court powers to the district judge. Although there could be no appeal to a circuit court, appeals from the district court could be taken to the Supreme Court. Capital cases were a significant exception: until 1889 there was no appeal of a conviction for a capital crime in any federal court, and the sentence of death by the district judge was final.

A congressional report of 1874 described the Western District of Arkansas as "a peculiar district," the only one with circuit court powers and common-law powers. The report also noted that the Fort Smith court's common-law jurisdiction was confined to cases coming to it from the Indian country, whereas its authority within Arkansas was the same as that of other federal tribunals, that is, based on both common and statutory law.

Not only did a condemned person have no recourse to a higher court, but the law mandated the death penalty (until 1897, the year after Parker's death) for anyone found guilty in a federal court of murder or rape. It was, however, possible for condemned murderers and rapists to seek a commutation to life imprisonment from the president of the United States. Also possible, but less common, was a presidential pardon. For the lesser crime of manslaughter, the maximum punishment was a three-year prison term; in 1875 Congress increased it to ten years. Similarly, in 1888, Congress raised the maximum penalty for larceny, burglary, or robbery in the Indian country to fifteen years or a fine of up to one thousand dollars, or both; previously, the maximum had been one year's incarceration. In 1887 Congress added adultery, incest, and fornication to the list of crimes in territories subject to federal authority; a federal law against bigamy had been on the books since 1862.

Federal courts in Arkansas were already ordering the death sentence for those committing capital crimes in the Indian Territory before Isaac Parker's tenure. The court at Little Rock sent several men to the gallows prior to 1851. Daniel Ringo assumed his duties as judge of the Western District in 1851, and in the following year he sentenced at least three people to hanging, with more to follow. The Arkansas press applauded Ringo's apparent determination to punish Indian Territory wrongdoers. Editorializing on the 1852 murder convictions, the *Arkansas Gazette* of December 17 expressed the hope that the hangings "will have a salutary influence upon the vicious [element] of that country, and [criminals] learn that the murder of white men will be followed with speedy justice."

Indian Territory residents were less enthusiastic about the new federal court in Van Buren. They continued to insist that a federal court be situated within Indian Territory boundaries. Congress, however, paid no heed. Instead, it broadened the Van Buren court's jurisdiction to include more offenses and enlarged its purview by adding other Arkansas counties. In 1864 Henry C. Caldwell, one of nineteenth-century America's most able jurists, succeeded Ringo as judge of the Eastern and Western Districts. In the twenty years from 1851 to 1871 during which the court for the Western District was at Van Buren, nine people received death sentences, but six succeeded in having their sentences commuted; of these, one was released by Confederate soldiers and another was pardoned.

A congressional act of March 3, 1871, moved the Western District Court from Van Buren to Fort Smith and added nineteen more counties to the district. In 1872 the commissioner of Indian affairs made a recommendation that an annual session of the court be held at Okmulgee, Indian Territory, but it was never acted on. During Parker's time, court was held only at Fort Smith. Legislation of 1877 and 1886 reduced the district to a compact group of counties, all in the western edge of Arkansas. The 1877 law increased the annual terms of the court from two to four, with terms to begin on the first Monday in February, May, August, and November.

Because of its Indian Territory jurisdiction, the Fort Smith court's caseload consisted mostly of criminal actions. Other federal courts, by contrast, heard mainly civil actions. Relatively few crimes were defined by federal statutes; most crimes—including the great majority of crimes for which Indian Territory defendants were tried—fell instead under the jurisdiction of common law. As a result, the relative lack of federal precedents in criminal law gave the judge of the Western District of Arkansas considerable latitude and freedom to break new ground.

Bowing to the wishes of the people of western Arkansas, the 1871 statute also provided the Fort Smith tribunal with a judge of its own. President Grant appointed William Story to the position, but it proved an unfortunate choice. According to historian Jeffrey Burton, Story was "endowed with a celerity of thought and suppleness of ethics that would not have put him apart from the rest of the Arkansas carpetbag class."

Yet Story's credentials appear impressive. Born in Wisconsin, he was the great-nephew of the eminent Justice Joseph Story of the United States Supreme Court. The younger Story was educated in Massachusetts, and after graduating from the University of Michigan's prestigious school of law in 1864, he served in a Wisconsin regiment until the close of the Civil War. After practicing law briefly in Milwaukee, he moved to Arkansas, where at the age of twenty-seven he was appointed judge of the state's Eighth, and later the Second, circuit courts.

Though recent scholarship has done much to discredit the view of carpetbaggers as scoundrels, Story's career lends a degree of support to the older interpretation. It was widely believed in Arkansas that the young jurist was soon to marry the daughter of United States Senator Alexander McDonald and that McDonald had engineered the creation of a separate judgeship for the Western District to provide a suitable position for his prospective son-in-law. If so, the senator and his daughter were disappointed; Story married another woman. It was Story's official conduct, however, that proved his undoing. Even before he took his place on the bench, concerned citizens of Arkansas, authorities in the Justice and Treasury departments, and members of Congress began noticing the astronomical costs of operating the Fort Smith tribunal. The increased activity of the court in the Indian Territory after the war partly explained the rising expenditures, but too many of the disbursements were not legitimate.

For all his shortcomings, Story was not the only culprit, nor even the worst. That dubious honor must be shared by the men who held the position of United States marshal. Others who were culpable included district attorneys; lesser court officials, such as deputy marshals and commissioners; and local businessmen who trafficked in discounted checks payable to witnesses and jurors. While the court was still in Van Buren, Marshal William Britton and some of his deputies were padding their accounts. Although Britton was removed from office, his replacement, former Arkansas congressman Logan H. Roots, was no improvement, and highly questionable expenditures for running the marshal's office continued to soar. At the request of Attorney General George H. Williams, President Grant suspended Roots and replaced him with, of all people, Britton, even though the Department of Justice had attempted to indict him for fraud. The Senate rejected Britton's nomination, and John N. Sarber succeeded as marshal in 1873.

Corruption was so rife in the Western District of Arkansas that in late 1872 the Treasury Department, at the attorney general's request, sent a Secret Service agent to Fort Smith. Operating under cover, Agent L. B. Whitney was able to report many examples of corruption, despite the fact that Story was aware of the agent's identity and that the Fort Smith postmaster was reading Whitney's mail and reporting the contents to Story and others being investigated.

The malfeasance that Agent Whitney uncovered was chiefly in the form of fees paid to deputy marshals for unnecessary travel in the Indian Territory and vouchers approved by the marshal and the judge for services rendered by nonexistent persons or persons who were unaware of their "services" and who never received a cent. Moreover, accusations of bribery and extortion were leveled against the judge, district attorney, marshal, and deputies.

The "expenses, disbursements, and general management" of the district court for the period during which Britton, Roots, and Sarber held the office of marshal was the subject of an inquiry by the House of Representative's Committee on Expenditures in the Department of Justice. The report on the inquiry, which covered the years 1871 to 1873, contained 316 pages of testimony that disclosed many irregularities and concluded that the expenditures had been "extraordinarily large." The report also noted Story's practice of allowing bail for convicted felons who were awaiting sentencing for capital offenses. Congress declined to act on the committee's recommendation that the court for the Western District of Arkansas be abolished. Nevertheless, the investigation hastened the departure of William Story. In return for Story's resignation, dated June 17, 1874, Attorney General Williams agreed to drop charges against him. The disgraced jurist soon left Arkansas, and later in the century he became the lieutenant governor of Colorado. Whether Story was truly corrupt or only a young man unable to cope with a difficult situation, the people of Arkansas were pleased to be rid of him. Pending the appointment of a new judge for the Western District, Henry C. Caldwell, judge of the Eastern District, returned to double duty, holding court in Little Rock and Fort Smith.

In 1874 the attorney general enlisted the services of Benjamin Du Val, a prominent Fort Smith lawyer, to investigate further the continuing mess in the Western District of Arkansas. As special assistant to the United States attorney for the district, Du Val prepared a damning report of 156 pages. He also pressured the district attorney and Sarber, the marshal, into resigning. William Henry Harrison Clayton, younger brother of Republican Senator Powell Clayton, became district attorney, and James F. Fagan became marshal. Meanwhile, a grand jury failed to indict Britton, Roots, and Sarber.

Thus, in the eight years preceding Parker's arrival as judge for the Western District of Arkansas, five marshals and three district attorneys had been removed from office. Given the defective laws providing for their compensation, court officials faced much temptation for dishonest accounting. The marshal and the district attorney each received a nominal annual salary of two hundred dollars, supplemented only by fees. Deputy marshals, in return for considerable risk of life, received only fees: two dollars for "service of any warrant, attachment, summons, capias, or other writs," and varying rates for "execution, venire, or summons or subpoena for a witness." If a deputy killed a suspect, he received nothing.

The law allowed a deputy marshal to employ up to three persons as *posse comitatus* to assist him. Posse members recruited in the Indian Territory were usually tough men who performed their tasks for the pay—three dollars a day—rather than as a civic duty.

The deputy was also entitled to payment for mileage—ten cents a mile, one way, "for himself, for each prisoner and necessary guard." A deputy could also collect fifty cents for contacting the first witness and thirty-seven cents for all others. Because many people were reluctant to serve as witnesses, the deputy sometimes received little or nothing for his efforts to track them down.

Out of the sums a deputy collected, the marshal legally was allowed to deduct at least one-fourth for his fee (Britton and Roots extracted one-third). Seldom did a deputy draw more than five hundred dollars a year; fifteen hundred dollars was as much as he could earn honestly. Even deputies who submitted truthful claims for payment frequently learned that zealous auditors in the Treasury and Justice departments in Washington had disallowed them.

There were opportunities, however, for deputies to collect rewards offered by local and state governments, private citizens, banks, railroads, and express companies. The federal government also paid rewards for the apprehension of mail robbers and murderers of federal employees, but the deputies were not entitled to this source of extra income because the government reasoned that they had already received federal money for capturing the criminals.

Throughout his tenure on the Fort Smith bench, Parker argued for a better system of compensation for these men, who worked under conditions far more difficult and hazardous than their counterparts in the more settled parts of the country. Without the deputy marshals, he declared, "I could not hold court a single day." Moreover, he argued, regular and adequate payment was imperative in order to attract a better class of people to carry out the difficult and dangerous work required of deputies working in the Indian Territory. In

1884 a bill was introduced in Congress to replace the fee system with salaries of $3,000 for the marshal and $1,200 for his chief deputy; the current marshal, Thomas Boles, asked that the salaries be fixed at $5,000 and $1,800, respectively. Unfortunately, the bill and the request were rejected, and the system remained essentially unreformed throughout the nineteenth century. Small wonder that allegations of abuses persisted even after Parker replaced the scoundrels surrounding Judge Story with upright and capable officers.

Parker moved quickly to counteract the continuing unfairness of the laws governing the payment of marshals and their deputies and the resultant temptation to add to their incomes by questionable means. He and his marshals carefully went over all applications for deputy marshal, doing their best to commission only the most qualified and trustworthy. Given the nature of the deputies' work, it is not surprising that many had rough edges and failed to meet the standards of conduct demanded of them. For example, one deputy bringing prisoners to Fort Smith halted at Purcell, in the Chickasaw Nation, for a break from his arduous duties. He and some friends got drunk and began discharging their pistols, resulting in ejection from a brothel, after which another rowdy shot him dead. The deputy's killer was tracked down and killed.

Some of the lawmen drifted over into the outlaw life. In 1877 Samuel Galpin, chief clerk of the Indian Office in Washington, expressed the belief that "many of these deputies should be brought to trial before the court rather than permitted longer to act as officers protected by its authority." Galpin charged that, too frequently, deputies ignored horse thieves and other dangerous outlaws and instead concentrated on violators of the liquor laws, often bringing them into court on trumped-up charges. Parker himself regularly brought instances of misconduct by deputies to the attention of the Justice Department. Nevertheless, the lawmen appointed during Parker's years on the Fort Smith bench were, on the whole, a decided improvement over those who had served earlier. Morale and esprit de corps improved accordingly. Near the end of his life, in a jury charge, Parker expressed his appreciation of the deputies: "Without these officers what is the use of this court? It takes men who are brave to uphold the law here."

Soon after assuming his judgeship, Parker authorized an increase in the number of deputy marshals. Most accounts say he immediately approved the appointment of two hundred deputies, but Juliet Galonska, park historian of the Fort Smith National Historic Site, calculates that there were no more than forty or fifty at any time. Anyone receiving an appointment as deputy marshal signed a written oath to "faithfully execute all lawful precepts, directed to the Marshal of the United States for the Western District of Arkansas, under authority of the United States, and true returns make and in all things well and truly, and without malice or partiality, perform the duties of Deputy Marshal of the Western District of Arkansas during my continuance in said office, and take only my lawful fees, so help me God."

Over the twenty-one years of Parker's tenure, these deputies captured or killed outlaws, recruited and led posses, served process and other documents issued under the authority of the court, and generally did what they could to keep the peace in the Indian Territory. Most took pride in being numbered among "the men who rode for Parker," though many of them paid for the honor with their lives. The number of deputies who died in the line of duty is traditionally given as sixty-five, a figure Parker supplied in an interview shortly before his death. According to Galonska, the number is more likely seventy-five to one hundred.

It should also be pointed out that the deputies "rode for," that is, served under, the marshal, not the judge. Parker told a jury that the lawmen acted for an even higher authority; deputies and their posses did not go out in the name of the court, but rather "in the name of the chief executive officer, the President of the United States." As historian Larry D. Ball has pointed out, however, the offices of the judge and marshal at Fort Smith were in closer physical proximity than at most other federal courts, which may have enabled the forceful Parker to exert more influence over the marshal and his deputies than did judges in other jurisdictions.

Each deputy received a booklet of rules and regulations informing him that

> U.S. Deputy Marshals for the Western District of Arkansas may make arrests for
> MURDER, MANSLAUGHTER,
> ASSAULT, WITH INTENT TO KILL OR TO MAIM,
> ATTEMPTS TO MURDER,
> ARSON, ROBBERY, RAPE, BURGLARY,
> LARCENY, INCEST, ADULTERY,
> WILFULLY AND MALICIOUSLY PLACING OBSTRUCTIONS
> ON A RAILROAD TRACK

The booklet explained that for the above offenses, a warrant was desirable but not required. For other infractions, such as violations of the revenue laws or introducing liquor into the Indian country, a warrant was necessary unless the culprit was caught in the act. The deputies were also instructed about the categories of crimes for which an Indian could be arrested.

The deputies hired teams and wagons to transport prisoners back to Fort Smith and to carry food and camping supplies. Before the Indian Territory and Fort Smith were connected by rail, the wagons had to be ferried across the Arkansas River. At night the lawmen shackled their charges to the wagon wheels or trees.

Henry Andrew "Heck" Thomas is considered by many to have been the finest example of a deputy marshal of the Western District court. He quickly gained a reputation for bravery and efficiency after entering the service of the Fort Smith court in 1886, and he faithfully served until 1892.

Thomas was one of several deputies who pursued the notorious Cherokee outlaw Ned Christie. Christie was a horse thief, a whiskey seller, and a cold-blooded killer. In 1889, Thomas and another deputy cornered Christie, and in the ensuing battle, Thomas shot Christie in the face. The outlaw managed to escape and in later skirmishes wounded three deputies and ambushed and killed another. In 1892, sixteen deputies, led by Heck Bruner and G. S. White, tracked Christie down to his sturdy log fort at the mouth of a canyon near Tahlequah. When rifle fire failed to dislodge Christie and a confederate, Marshal Jacob Yoes personally took command and obtained a cannon, which too proved inadequate. The lawmen finally forced Christie from his stronghold with dynamite and gunned him down.

The careers of the Dalton brothers illustrate the often thin line that separated lawmen and outlaws. Frank Dalton was a respected deputy of the Fort Smith court who, in 1887, while attempting to arrest three whiskey sellers, was cut down. Marshal John Carroll appointed Frank's brother Grat as his replacement. Grat employed two other brothers, Bob and Emmett, as possemen; Bob later accepted a commission as deputy. While still in the service of the court, the three Daltons began their criminal careers, initially as horse thieves. After quitting as deputies, they formed, in Glenn Shirley's words, "the most desperate band of robbers to infest the Indian Territory." They added bank robbery, train holdups, and murder to their list of crimes. Grat and Bob Dalton and others of their outlaw band did not live long enough to be hauled before Isaac C. Parker. They and other members of the gang were shot down by citizens of Coffeyville, Kansas, while attempting to rob two of the town's banks in broad daylight. Emmett Dalton, who was wounded in the fray, served a long prison term.

Other deputies who earned reputations for bravery and devoted service included Paden Tolbert, J. H. Mershon, James F. "Bud" Ledbetter, David V. Rusk, and Wesley Bowman. Reflecting the diverse population of the Indian Territory, the corps of deputies included Indians, mixed-bloods, blacks and whites, and veterans of both the blue and the gray.

Even with the recruitment of good deputies such as Thomas, and the determined efforts of Parker and the district attorneys, curbing criminality in the Indian Territory was nearly impossible. Among the factors contributing to the continuing difficulties were its remoteness and its size—the combined area of the territory and the Arkansas counties amounting to 74,000 square miles.

The exploits of federal lawmen in the Indian Territory have helped create a misconception about United States marshals as gun-toting law enforcement officers of the American West. In reality, all federal courts, even the United States Supreme Court, have had a marshal, as provided for in the Judiciary Act of 1789. Only in relatively unsettled areas such as Arizona and New Mexico territories—and most conspicuously, the Indian Territory—were marshals concerned mainly with bringing outlaws to justice. In the states, law enforcement was largely the province of local and state officials.

Rather than someone who, six-shooter at his side, saddled up and rode out in search of desperadoes, a federal marshal was primarily an administrative officer of the court. He was required to carry out all lawful orders of the judges, Congress, and the president. The marshal was likewise responsible for the serving of writs, warrants, subpoenas, summonses, and other process. In addition, his work involved a great deal of bookkeeping: submitting estimates of court expenses to Congress and paying the fees and expenses of the clerk, United States attorney, jurors, witnesses, and his deputies. Other responsibilities included attending court sessions, calling up prospective jurors, delivering prisoners to jails and penitentiaries, overseeing the execution of those convicted of capital crimes, and supervising the deputy marshals. The latter included not only the field deputies, but also those who worked in his office. The office deputies tallied fines that had been collected, paid expenses incurred by the court, and helped maintain records. Until 1870 the marshals also took the national census.

Seven men served as marshals of Parker's court, beginning with James F. Fagan. Replacing him in 1876 was another Grant appointee, D. P. Upham. Upham, a native of Massa-

chusetts, was one of many northerners who came south after
the Civil War in search of economic and political rewards. He
settled in Woodward County, in eastern Arkansas, and made
money in merchandising, real estate, and the cotton business.
In politics, he served in the legislature as a Radical Republican. When the Ku Klux Klan launched a reign of terror,
Arkansas Governor Powell Clayton declared martial law.
Upham helped organize a militia force in Woodward County,
and in 1868 Governor Clayton appointed him commander of
the district of northeastern Arkansas. Under his leadership,
black and white militiamen engaged the Klan in a number of
armed clashes. His stern measures against the Klan played a
major role in its suppression in the state. In 1869 Governor
Clayton ended martial law, and Upham returned to more
peaceable pursuits, but not without having earned the abiding hatred of many whites in his area.

Parker welcomed Upham's appointment as marshal: "As
fine a man as ever I saw. He is honored by all except Ku Klux,
thieves, gamblers, drunkards and liars." As marshal, Upham
assisted Parker in rooting out corruption in the court. To
relieve the dreary existence of the prisoners in his charge and
to benefit the community, Upham put some of them to work
on the streets of Fort Smith and the grounds surrounding the
courthouse. When Congress failed to appropriate sufficient
funds for the court, he contributed money from his own
pocket to keep it in operation. He remained in office until
1880, when Republican Senator Stephen W. Dorsey brought
about his removal.

Upham's successor, appointed by President Rutherford B.
Hayes, was Valentine Dell, who owned the Republican newspaper, the *Fort Smith New Era*, and was an early supporter of
Parker. Dell, however, incurred Parker's displeasure. The
judge found him "ill natured, irascible and impractical . . . a
friend of bad and reckless men who only want an opportunity to filch money from the government." Dell also ran afoul
of Powell Clayton, who had moved from the governorship to
the United States Senate in 1871. Dell served as marshal only

from 1880 to 1882. A more satisfactory appointment, from Parker's standpoint, was a former Republican congressman from Arkansas, Thomas Boles, selected by President Chester A. Arthur. Boles was an ally of Senator Clayton.

The first administration of Grover Cleveland brought a Democrat, John Carroll, to the office of marshal. Despite the party difference and the fact that he was a former Confederate colonel, Carroll worked well with Parker. The election of Benjamin Harrison put the Fort Smith marshalcy back into Republican hands with the appointment of Jacob Yoes. Parker's last marshal was Democrat George J. Crump, chosen by Cleveland during his second presidential term. Like Carroll, Crump's party affiliation presented no apparent problems in his relations with Republican jurist Parker.

The other major court officer was the United States District Attorney, the person who prosecuted those accused of crime. This official also represented the United States in civil actions in which the government was a party. The man who held this position for over half of Parker's tenure was William H. H. Clayton. Although William Clayton owed his job to the influence of his brother, Senator Powell Clayton, he was an earnest advocate who faithfully represented the government. He and the judge enjoyed a harmonious and mutually supportive relationship. Parker praised the zealous prosecutor as a "very close, shrewd, prudent examiner of witnesses." In the mid-1880s, Clayton was replaced by Democrat M. H. Sandals, an appointee of President Cleveland. The Republican administration of Benjamin Harrison returned Clayton to the post in 1889. The second Cleveland presidency gave the job to James F. Read.

In his first month in office, Parker appealed successfully to the United States attorney general for funds to hire assistant district attorneys. The first were James Brizzolara and George A. Grace; followed by J. B. Forrester in the later 1880s; then William M. Mellette and Edward J. Fannin; and J. B. McDonough and Edgar Smith in the early 1890s. Yearly salaries for the assistant district attorneys ranged from one

William H. H. Clayton, United States District Attorney during most of Parker's tenure as judge at Fort Smith. *Archives and Manuscripts Division, Oklahoma Historical Society.*

thousand to two thousand dollars. Parker continually asked the Department of Justice for higher pay for his court officials.

Like the marshal, the district attorney received a nominal salary of two hundred dollars per year, with the bulk of his income derived from fees. United States district attorneys and marshals served four-year terms, after which they were subject to removal and replacement with someone of the president's political persuasion. They could have their commissions revoked before the end of the term, but this was usually in cases of gross malpractice or inability to carry out the duties of the office.

Another long-time Parker colleague was the clerk of the district court, Stephen Wheeler, a native of New York. Like William H. H. Clayton, Wheeler had served with distinction as a Union army officer. Prior to joining the Parker court, he had been quartermaster general of the Arkansas militia and state auditor. For a brief time at the beginning of Parker's tenure, there were clerks for the circuit and district courts at Fort Smith, with Wheeler as circuit clerk and Eugene L. Stephenson as district clerk; by 1877, Wheeler was the clerk of both courts. Since the appointment of the clerk was the judge's prerogative, Wheeler was able to survive Democratic administrations in Washington and remain in his post even after Parker died. His compensation consisted entirely of fees.

For many years Wheeler was also one of the many United States commissioners attached to the court. These officials were lawyers who served part-time and for fees only. A commissioner's primary responsibilities were to issue writs and to conduct preliminary hearings to determine if a suspected lawbreaker should be bound over for trial in regular court. They were found in several communities in northwestern Arkansas, such as Dardanelle, Eureka Springs, Fayetteville, Fort Smith, Van Buren, and Yellville. Others were located in the Indian Territory: Fort Sill, Muskogee, Okmulgee, Tahlequah, and elsewhere. Among those who served as commissioners for many years were James Brizzolara, L. C. Hall, E. B. Harrison, George O. Limbarger, and Jesse Turner.

The commissioners were potentially advantageous to a busy district court because they could dispense of many cases, thereby reducing the court's caseload. Parker, however, cut the number of commissioners in Arkansas and eliminated them altogether in the Indian Territory by 1889. Doing away with the commissioners in the territory aroused protests. Parker answered that, rather than reducing his caseload, the commissioners added to his burden. "If commissioners are scattered over the Indian country," he wrote, "the annoyance to the people will be much greater than it is by their having to come to Fort Smith, as they will suffer increased annoyance because of frivolous, unnecessary, and improper prosecutions." One scholar, Jeffrey Burton, a close student of the judicial history of the Indian Territory, has offered a more plausible explanation of the judge's action: "Perhaps Parker, a man of prodigious stamina and no small vanity, merely thought it intolerable that important antejudicial proceedings in his district should be held out of his earshot." Another probable reason for the decline and eventual elimination of commissioners in the territory was the reduction of the Fort Smith court's jurisdiction in the 1880s.

In addition to the marshal and deputies, district attorney and assistants, clerk, and commissioners, other staff rounded out the personnel of the court: a register in bankruptcy, a stenographer, bailiffs, a messenger, a janitor, a jailer, and guards. For many years Jacob G. Hammersly served as the court's crier, opening its proceedings with: "Oyez! Oyez! The Honorable District Court of the United States for the Western District of Arkansas, having criminal jurisdiction of the Indian Territory, is now in session. God bless the United States and this Honorable Court."

Also serving the court were those who sat, for three dollars a day, as members of the grand and petit juries. Jury duty took people away from work and family, often for extended periods. Given the relatively small population base from which jurors were selected, many of them performed this obligation often. Parker was mindful of the burden and inconvenience involved and appreciated the civic-mindedness of those who were called as jurors for his court. He expressed this admiration well in a letter to a boy, Argyle Langston, who had written complaining that jury duty had kept his father away from home too long. The judge assured the boy that his father would return soon, adding, "You know your father is a good man, and we need good men to make up the juries. . . . I hope I may live long to see you become a useful man like your father. I was very glad to get your note and you will give my kind regards to your mother and you will believe me to be Most truly your friend, I. C. Parker."

While the judge praised the jurors, Henry Starr, a desperado whom Parker's juries had twice convicted of murder, had a different view: "Arkansas is noted for ignorance and Hill-Billyism, and fifty percent of the jurymen were drawn from backwoods counties and were completely dominated by the powerful personality of Judge Parker."

One of the welcome changes Parker brought about was payment of jurors and witnesses in cash rather than discounted scrip. This payment made the citizens of Parker's jurisdiction more willing to serve as jurymen and to appear as witnesses. After the Parker court had been in operation for a few years, a local newspaper remarked that "Everything seems to work like well oiled machinery. Every officer and employee is found at his post, alert and efficient in his particular calling."

Yet Parker almost got off on the wrong foot by attempting to secure the appointment of his brother-in-law, Thomas B. Burnett, as special federal prosecutor. Without mentioning his relationship with Burnett, Parker assured Attorney General Edwards Pierrepoint that "a good accountant" was needed to complete the supposedly unfinished business of special assistant Benjamin Du Val's investigation of corruption in the district court. Fortunately for Parker, the effort failed and did not become public knowledge. Had the people of the district learned of the attempt, it would have caused many Arkansans to suspect that the new judge was no better than his discredited predecessor, William Story.

Parker was correct, however, in saying that some matters had eluded Du Val. A few weeks after Parker took his place on the bench, Pierrepoint called Parker to Washington to explain accounts totaling near forty thousand dollars that the judge had approved. Parker and a United States senator from Arkansas testified that the amount was justifiable.

Even with honest officials, the Fort Smith court continued to be expensive. In 1878, 1879, and 1887, the court had to suspend business temporarily because it ran out of funds. The court for the Western District of Arkansas was not alone in feeling a financial pinch; Congress was niggardly with appropriations for other tribunals even though the system of federal courts was rapidly expanding in size and need for money. The attorneys general responded to Parker's frequent appeals for additional money with admonitions to economize.

Pending the location of a permanent courthouse, the first court sessions at Fort Smith under Judge Story were held at the privately owned Rogers Building, which was subsequently destroyed by fire in 1872. After briefly meeting in the Sebastian County courthouse, Story's court moved in November 1872 to a structure belonging to the abandoned military post of Fort Smith, a two-story brick building that had been a barracks for enlisted men. The courtroom was located in the northeast room on the ground floor of the old barracks. Other rooms were converted into a jury room and offices for the marshal, district attorney, clerk, and other court personnel. The courtroom was furnished with tables and chairs for the attorneys, witnesses, and prisoners, and a gallery for spectators. The judge sat on a leather-bottomed, high-backed chair behind a large, cherry-paneled desk. When Parker took over, he maintained his chambers in the former commissary building of the fort. The arrangement was adequate but by no means ideal.

Far worse was a facility situated in the basement beneath the court building: the jail. Before the establishment of the court at Fort Smith, prisoners of the Western District were housed, at federal expense, in the Arkansas state penitentiary at Little Rock or local jails. The United States district attorney for the Eastern District of Arkansas, in an 1876 report, noted the deplorable conditions at the penitentiary. He pointed out that the federal prisoners kept there "are usually from the western district of this State, and the conviction has cost the Government several thousand dollars in each case, when the sordid system of imprisonment existing in Arkansas turns them loose upon the public, in a condition of outlawry, worse foes to society than before their prosecution."

The establishment of the separate court for the Western District meant a new home for its prisoners. The Fort Smith jail, certainly no improvement over the Little Rock facility, was a two-cell affair in the basement of the courthouse which had been used as a kitchen when the building was a barracks. Everyone, including Parker, agreed that it was entirely unsuitable, indeed a disgrace. It was damp, poorly ventilated, lacking in the most basic sanitary facilities, and usually packed with 75 to 150 inmates. In general, the men kept there were awaiting trial or execution or were serving brief sentences for minor offenses. Sick and healthy; black, Indian, and white inmates led a miserable coexistence. As the 1884 report of the attorney general noted: "as there are but two large rooms in which to confine the prisoners, nothing separates the outlaw and the murderer from the detained witness. Young and old, innocent and guilty, are all crowded together." The next year, the attorney general wrote feelingly of "what is commonly dignified by the title of the 'United States jail,' but which is in reality little better than a pen" and a "standing reproach." He exonerated the marshal from blame: "[I]t is not his fault that he is the nominal warden of the most miserable prison, probably in the whole country."

A wall separated the two rooms or cells of the basement. Each cell measured fifty-five feet long, twenty-nine feet wide, and seven feet high. The floors were covered with flagstones, and the outer walls of stone were two and a half feet thick.

The cells each had four front windows measuring six feet, four inches in height, and four smaller rear windows. Both cells had front doors six feet, three inches high and four feet wide, covered with heavy wood shutters on the inside and iron bars on the outside. Behind each door was a small room built of wood, which opened into the cell. According to Marshal Thomas Boles, the rooms "were built as a protection to the front doors and to prevent a rush being made by the inmates upon the turnkeys." They also served as areas where prisoners could consult their attorneys. Two small rear doors were always kept shut.

Within the cells were coal-oil barrels sawed in half and used for bathing. Slop tubs and tubs for human waste were removed twice a day and emptied into pits outside the walls of the fort. The jailer's "office" was a wooden shanty; the prisoners' belongings were kept there and in the courthouse attic. A small brick structure seventy-five yards from the jail, formerly the post guardhouse, served as a place of confinement for the few female prisoners. Also seventy-five yards from the facility was a "little old board house" where the cooking and washing were done.

Although a physician visited regularly, an alarming number of inmates contracted serious diseases. "[I]t is only with the most rigid and vigilant attention to [the jail's] cleanliness," reported Boles, "and the free use of disinfectants, principally in the shape of lime, that I have been able to keep up the good health of its inmates." There was also constant fear of contagious diseases, especially smallpox. When the weather was not too hot, the marshal sometimes moved sick prisoners to an attic room of the courthouse.

In 1885 a grand jury charged by Parker with inspecting and reporting on conditions at the jail sent its predictable recommendations to the judge. The jurors found it "entirely wrong" that "boys and those charged with misdemeanors" were "incarcerated in the same cell with murderers and desperadoes of hardened character." They also urged the construction of separate quarters for sick prisoners. On a positive note, they observed that the jail was "neat and clean and in a satisfactory condition, as far as it is possible for it to be made so." The food appeared to be "good and wholesome and supplied in abundance." Under the circumstances, the jurors were satisfied "that a careful and intelligent supervision is exercised over this department." The head jailer, Charles Burns, began service under Marshals Roots and Sarber and continued, with a four-year interruption, until 1882. Usually in vain did Parker beg the Justice Department for funds to hire more guards.

The Department of Justice contracted with a number of state and local prisons to house long-term federal prisoners. The best known and most progressive was the Detroit House of Correction. In 1884 the attorney general informed Congress that "the report of the house of correction, where prisoners sentenced in the western district of Arkansas are confined, shows that a large number of the deaths in that institution is made up of convicts who were confined in the Fort Smith jail previous to their trial and sentence." Other prisons housing inmates convicted in Parker's court were located in Joliet, Pontiac, and Menard, Illinois; Moundsville, West Virginia; Columbus, Ohio; Brooklyn and Albany, New York; Cheltenham and Baltimore, Maryland; Little Rock, Arkansas; and Anamosa, Iowa.

Only the penitentiaries at Menard and Detroit met Parker's standards, because they emphasized rehabilitation and education. In 1885 he informed Attorney General Augustus H. Garland that the others were "run on the purely speculative principle of getting the most dollars and cents out of the transaction by those who conduct them." He said that money as a consideration should be secondary to "the good of all men." In Parker's last months on the bench, several prisoners were sent or transferred to the new federal penitentiary at Leavenworth, Kansas.

Late in the century, Parker also sentenced youthful offenders to the federal reform school in Washington, D.C. When Attorney General Richard Olney questioned Parker's practice

of sending boys over the age of sixteen to reformatories rather
adult prisons, Parker replied: "When I consider that these lads
are generally made criminals by their environment, the temptation is quite strong for me to not be very particular about
the matter of age." He expressed the wish that there were "a
reform school to which we could send all young criminals, for
I believe most of them can be saved by proper treatment and
proper surroundings."

Because the means of providing for the inmates' physical
well-being were inadequate, the keepers of the Fort Smith jail
hoped to offset this problem with efforts to tend to their spir-
itual needs. Each Sunday, local clergymen preached to the
prisoners, and the "Christian ladies" of the community
offered Sunday-school classes.

As the national notoriety of the court and judge at Fort
Smith grew, so did the infamy of the jail. In time, the government provided a much-improved facility. Meanwhile, the
dungeon below the courthouse became known as "Hell on
the Border."

In addition to inheriting an unprepossessing courthouse
and a squalid jail, Parker faced the responsibility of overhaul-
ing a court plagued with corruption and incompetence. The
new judge also had to win over the skeptical and potentially
hostile citizenry of Arkansas and the Indian Territory.
Because of the national reputation of the scandal-ridden
court over which he was to preside, it was imperative that he
convince the American public of his own rectitude. In short
order, he was to prove himself worthy of his position and of
the trust of those who had elevated him to the federal bench.

CHAPTER 3

I Never Hanged a Man

PARKER, a seasoned politician, knew how to establish friendly ties with the people of Fort Smith. From the beginning, he cultivated the local press, and he soon had the support of the Democratic newspapers, the *Western Independent* and the *Fort Smith Weekly Herald*, as well as the Republican *Fort Smith Weekly New Era*. As befitted a federal jurist, Parker avoided public involvement in partisan matters. Soon after arriving in Fort Smith, Parker implied to a *Herald* reporter that he found the community to his liking and intended to reside there permanently. Throughout his life in Arkansas, the judge proved adept at getting favorable press attention, not only locally, but also from papers in Kansas, Missouri, and New York.

The Parker family's involvement in community affairs did much to win over the people of the town. One of Parker's chief contributions to the betterment of his adopted community was furthering the cause of public education. For several years he sat as member and sometime president of the school board. Apart from having two sons who attended the Fort Smith schools, his commitment to education stemmed from his belief that there would be fewer criminals if young people were instructed properly in the responsibilities of citizenship. Speaking of the majority of the criminal defendants who appeared in his court, he was of the opinion that: "The want of proper training, ignorance, bad associates and bad advice, in my experience with these kind of people, have more to do with making them criminals than natural wickedness and inherited depravity." As one local journalist put it: "[I]f he had done nothing else at all," Parker's work for improving the school system "was sufficient to entitle him to lasting recognition at the hands of the people of Fort Smith." Several years later, Parker went to Washington to lobby for a bill to grant federal land to Fort Smith for its schools.

Parker was the main speaker at Fort Smith's celebration of the nation's centennial on July 4, 1876. His address praised the "principle[s] of American freedom and American equality." He lauded the national unity brought about by the Civil War and the war's other great result, the end of slavery.

In 1887 Parker became one of the founding members of the board of trustees of Saint John's Hospital. He was also instrumental in establishing a library and organizing the county fair. His name was associated with several local charities. Fraternal associations that claimed him as a member included the Independent Order of Odd Fellows and the Knights of Honor. The latter was organized by members of the Odd Fellows and the Ancient Order of United Workmen in 1873. Its main purpose was to offer brotherly unity and assistance to white males of good morals and health. Unlike the Odd Fellows and other fraternal and benevolent organizations, the Knights took no initiation oath; they promised only to abide by the regulations of the organization and to aid lodge members in need. Members were required to profess belief in a supreme being. Parker also belonged to the Union veterans' organization, the Grand Army of the Republic.

Some biographers have written that Parker affiliated himself with the Methodist church and remained a steadfast communicant, but more reliable sources state that although he read the Bible and firmly believed in the tenets of Christianity, he was not affiliated with any denomination. Mary, on the other hand, regularly attended Mass, and occasionally Parker accompanied her. Truly ecumenical, he numbered among his friends members of the town's Jewish community. He established especially close ties with merchant Isaac Cohn, and he officiated at Cohn and Fannie Silverberg's wedding in 1883.

The two men developed what has been described as a "loosely formed business relationship," which may also have included Green McCurtain, later the principal chief of the Choctaw Nation. In 1892, Parker was among the local dignitaries who attended the dedication of the synagogue erected by Fort Smith's United Hebrew Congregation.

A Fort Smith newspaper described Parker as "very sociable" and having "a pleasant smile and a kind word for everyone." He was uniformly democratic in his relations with citizens from all levels of society. "Even people to whom some public men would not think of speaking, Judge Parker stops and chats with in a friendly way." Once, during a recess of the court, as the judge was leaving for lunch, a particularly tough-looking fellow accosted him and "in a familiar way began questioning him about a case." Parker "stopped and placed his hand on the man's shoulder, answered the latter's questions and talked with him fully five minutes, as if he had been a highly honored citizen."

In his later years, a playmate of his granddaughter Lily Parker saw him as a kindly man who loved children. With his then-white hair and beard, he reminded the little girl of Santa Claus.

Parker immediately demonstrated uncommon energy in his handling of his court's crowded docket. Monday through Saturday, he heard cases from 8:00 A.M. until early evening. Sometimes proceedings lasted into the early morning hours. He once delivered a jury charge at 2:30 A.M. and reopened court at 8:00 A.M. as usual. Such dedication to duty did not impress everyone favorably, however. One prominent Fort Smith attorney made the caustic comment that Parker's "chief amusement" was holding court.

In his first eight years, Parker heard 2,398 criminal cases and 277 civil actions. The criminal cases resulted in 1,596 convictions. The cost came to almost $1.25 million, or about $700 per conviction. Small wonder that officials in Washington continued to balk at paying the court's expenses.

Earning the respect of the people of western Arkansas required more than being a solid citizen. Nor was it enough to prove that he was an honest and hardworking jurist who was intent upon cleaning up the corrupt conditions he had inherited. He had to show a determination to impose law and order in the Indian Territory.

Nothing could more have impressed upon the inhabitants of Arkansas and the Five Nations of the Indian Territory Parker's seriousness of purpose than the imposing of the death penalty for the most serious of crimes. His fame rests principally on his handing down the death sentence more often than any other American judge. In popular lore, he sent eighty-eight people to the gallows. This figure comes from the subtitle of the first book written about him, Samuel W. Harman's *Hell on the Border: He Hanged Eighty-Eight Men* (1898). There are two errors here. Harman miscounted; the real figure is seventy-nine. Also, Parker insisted, correctly, that he had hanged no one. Whenever a jury in his court found someone guilty of murder or rape, the judge had no choice but to impose the death penalty, as federal law mandated. As Parker himself put it in an oft-quoted remark: "I never hanged a man; it was the law."

Harman's figure of eighty-eight was an honest mistake. The same cannot be said of a statistic invented by Henry L. Dawes, who served in the House of Representatives with Parker and later became a United States senator. He was the chief sponsor of the Dawes Severalty Act of 1887, which allowed Indian reservations to be divided into allotments for individual Indians, with the surplus land to be opened up to non-Indians for homesteads. The act did not apply to the lands of the Five Nations, but in 1893 Congress created a commission, headed by Dawes, charged with attempting to persuade the Nations to agree to have their communal lands brought under the terms of the Dawes Act. Breaking up the communal lands would pave the way for statehood for the Indian and Oklahoma territories, a goal Dawes earnestly supported. In an effort to show the situation in the Indian Territory in the worst light, Dawes, in an 1896 address, singled out "One judge who has been there ten or fifteen years

[who] has sentenced something like 1,000 men to be hanged for crimes committed in that Territory." Dawes knew better; he had earlier asked the clerk of Parker's court for information on the number of death sentences handed down at Fort Smith, and the clerk had responded with a list of 172. Nevertheless, two published versions of Dawes's speech containing the outrageous falsehood were widely circulated.

Although Parker was bound by jury verdicts, his critics were quick to point out that the judge exercised undue influence over juries, guiding them to the conclusions he wanted. Though sensitive to unfair accusations that he enjoyed sending men to be hanged, he admitted that he did not passively preside over his court. When defense attorneys and others complained that he led juries, he candidly acknowledged that "juries have never failed me, they are willing to do their duty, but they must be led. They must know that the judge wants the enforcement of the law." Or, as he put it on another occasion: "Juries should be led. They have a right to expect that, and if guided will render that justice that is the greatest pillar of society." The defense lawyers also complained, not without cause, that he bullied their witnesses and coached those for the prosecution.

Although there were always several cases still pending at the end of a term, Parker moved business along briskly, disposing quickly of the many minor actions with which his docket was overloaded. Murder trials, however, merited a more deliberate pace, and he never confined these proceedings to a single day.

Had the will of the court been carried out in all instances during Parker's tenure, 161 persons would have been executed for their crimes. That less than half did is accounted for in various ways. The majority of the eighty-one eluded the hangman because the president of the United States commuted their sentences to life or to shorter terms; some of these were later pardoned. At least two received pardons before serving a sentence. Some died while awaiting sentencing or execution; others were killed trying to escape. Occasionally, men convicted of murder received new trials, after which they were discharged or found guilty of the noncapital crime of manslaughter.

Until 1889 there could be no appeal from Parker's court. That year Congress allowed appeals to the United States Supreme Court. Thereafter, several convictions for capital crimes were reversed. The resultant new trials in the lower court frequently ended with conviction for a lesser charge, acquittal, or nolle prosequi (a declaration by the district attorney that he would not further prosecute a case).

Hangings at Fort Smith occurred before Parker took his place on the bench. His predecessor Henry C. Caldwell sent at least one man to the gallows during his brief tenure as interim judge of the Western District in 1871. From 1873 to 1874, William Story sentenced seven men, all of them Indians or part-Indian, to be hanged, beginning with the execution of John Childers on August 15, 1873.

Parker took his place on the bench on May 10, 1875, one week after his arrival in Fort Smith. The most pressing duties before him were to address the cluttered state of affairs Judge Story had created and to turn the court into an efficient instrument of justice. Some of the problems antedated Story's tenure; for example, the court at Fort Smith had been unwilling or unable to give much attention to law enforcement in the Indian Territory during the Civil War and Reconstruction.

In his first term of court, Parker presided over the trials of eighteen men accused of murder. The jury found fifteen of them guilty. The judge sentenced eight of them to be executed on September 3, 1875. One of them, Frank Butler, attempted to escape and was brought down by the rifle of Deputy George Maledon. Another, Oscar Snow, because of his youth, received a commutation of his sentence from President Grant; later he was pardoned.

The remaining six condemned men were Daniel Evans, William J. Whittington, and James H. Moore (all three white); Smoker Mankiller and Samuel Fooy (both Indian); and Edmund "Heck" Campbell (black). Evans murdered a youth in the Creek Nation and made off with his horse, saddle, and boots. Whittington clubbed a man with whom he had been drinking, slashed his throat, and robbed him of $100 in the Chickasaw Nation. Moore, a horse thief, murdered a deputy marshal. Mankiller fatally shot a neighbor with a rifle he had borrowed from him. Fooy took the life of a young Cherokee Nation schoolteacher, John Emmit Neff, in order to steal the $250 Neff was carrying. Campbell killed a farmer and his mistress in the Choctaw Nation for no apparent motive.

After a lengthy charge from the judge and deliberating only a few minutes, the jury found Evans guilty. Parker gave the sullen killer a memorable scolding and, according to a newspaper account, told Evans, "I sentence you to hang by the neck until you are dead, dead, dead!" The condemned man responded with a sneer and an offhand "I thank ye, judge."

In handing down the sentences of the others, Parker sternly reproached them, as well. After reciting the grisly details of Whittington's heinous act, the judge went on to say: "But your guilt and your depravity did not stop there. Scarcely had you committed the bloody deed before you entered upon the commission of another crime. You converted to your person as spoils of the murder your victim's money."

He assured Smoker Mankiller that "the sword of human justice is about to fall upon your guilty head." Fooy's crime was made all the worse, he said, by sending "a soul unprepared to its Maker. You have set at defiance God's law." In the same biblical tones, after telling Campbell, "Your fate is inevitable," he added, "Let me, therefore, beg of you to fly to your Maker for that mercy and that pardon which you cannot expect from mortals . . . and endeavor to seize upon the salvation of the Cross." Parker bade the six men "Farewell forever until the court and you and all here today shall meet together in the general resurrection." A judge's use of biblical language such as this was common in Parker's time. There is no good evidence to support the often-repeated statement that he wept after delivering these or other death sentences.

On the south side of the old garrison's grounds, three hundred feet from the former commissary building which now housed Parker's chambers, stood the gallows. A reporter for a Saint Louis newspaper provided a full description of the scaffold:

The structure is built of rough timbers. The crossbeam is a stout piece of hewed oak, supported on two upright posts, very strongly braced. The platform is about seven feet from the ground. The distance between the supporting posts is about twelve feet, giving nearly two feet space for the fall of each victim. The trap extends across the breadth of the platform, and consists of two pieces strongly hinged to the flooring of the platform so that they form a connection in the nature of a double door when closed from below. These are held in place when brought up by a stout beam of oak, extending in the direction of the gallows' beam on which rest two arms firmly fastened to one flap of the door below. To this beam about the middle is secured an iron trigger bar which passes up through a place provided in the trap doors and is secured by a knee in a strong iron lever about three feet long, well secured on the facing of the platform floor. By a movement of this lever back, the trigger bar which holds the trap in position is released and the doors drop down. On this door the condemned men will stand. Six ropes . . . are tied over the beam, and six bags of sand of 200 pounds in weight each have been thrice dropped to test the further working of this awful enginery of death.

The gallows were designed to put six persons at a time to death. An enlarged gallows, built in 1886, could handle twelve. Only once more, however, in 1890, did as many as six "trap door angels" hang on one day. There were a few single executions, but most of the condemned were executed in groups of two to five.

All six men were to be hanged on the morning of the appointed day. A large number of spectators crowded into the grounds to witness the affair. At 9:30 the prisoners, attended by four clergymen and flanked by a dozen guards, were led from the jail wearing leg irons and handcuffs. They marched two abreast to the scaffold, where they sat on benches at the rear of the gallows. Marshal Fagan read their death warrants, with Smoker Mankiller's in Cherokee and English.

Each prisoner was asked if he had any last words. Evans defiantly shook his head. Moore announced that there were worse men than he in the crowd and expressed the hope that they "make peace with God before brought to my condition." Fooy announced that he was "as anxious to get out of this world as you are to see me go." Campbell proclaimed his innocence but also his readiness to die. He bade the spectators farewell, expressing the wish that "they would all meet in heaven." Mankiller, who spoke only Cherokee, told the onlookers through an interpreter that he, too, was innocent and that he stood before them "convicted by prejudice and false testimony."

In a statement read by one of the clergymen, Whittington acknowledged his guilt but placed the blame on the bad example set by his whiskey-drinking father: "I took to his practice and this is what has brought me to the gallows. When I got drunk I knew not what I was doing and so killed my best friend." He closed by crying out, "Oh! That men would leave off drinking altogether. And, O, parents, I send forth this dying warning to you today, standing on the gallows: *Train up your children the way they should go.* My father's example brought me to ruin. God save us all! Farewell! Farewell!"

After prayers and hymn-singing, the arms of the condemned men were bound and black hoods were placed over their heads. Hangman George Maledon adjusted the nooses around the head of each man. Following the preliminaries, Maledon pulled back the iron lever that released the trigger bar that caused the doors of the trap to fall. All six men met their end with broken necks. Just before the trap was sprung, Whittington cried out, "Jesus save me!"

On that day, September 3, the *Fort Smith Independent* published a twelve-inch by twelve-inch extra carrying news of the sensational event. A large column heading proclaimed, "Execution Day!!"; smaller ones announced that a "Large Crowd" had seen the "6 Murderers Hanged" and offered "Details of the Execution." Along with representatives of the local press, newspaper reporters from Saint Louis, Kansas City, Little Rock, and back east covered the affair, and news of the multiple execution traveled beyond Fort Smith and the Indian Territory. The dispatches described the proceedings in dramatic detail. Isaac C. Parker's reputation as the Hanging Judge was launched.

The first several hangings were attended by thousands of spectators, many of them from distant parts. A carnival air pervaded the proceedings, with hawkers dispensing liquor, soft drinks, edibles, and souvenirs. Parker found such an atmosphere distasteful, and in 1881, orders from the Justice Department stopped the public spectacle of hangings at Fort Smith. A stockade was put up around the gallows, leaving a space for only about forty onlookers, who were limited to those to whom passes had been issued—relatives of the condemned men, court officials, attorneys, and members of the press. Contrary to legend, Parker never witnessed the executions from the window of his chambers or anywhere else.

Among the court's personnel, George Maledon was second only to Parker in notoriety. Before becoming a hangman, he had served as a policeman in Fort Smith, a deputy sheriff for Sebastian County, and a guard at the jail underneath the federal courthouse. He would hang the majority of the men Parker sent to the scaffold. The German-born Maledon approached his grim work with appropriate seriousness and took pride in the success that usually attended his meticulous preparations. He favored ropes of handwoven hemp from Saint Louis, which he oiled and, to guard against slippage, impregnated with pitch.

Maledon was also a Union veteran, and in one of the rare instances when he did not hang someone sentenced to death in Parker's court, it was because he could not bear to execute a former Union soldier. There was nothing about the condemned man's crime that appealed to the hangman's sympathy—Shep Busby had killed a deputy who had come to arrest him for adultery—but Maledon asked the judge to excuse him from duty. Parker understood and assigned the task to Deputy Marshal G. S. White.

The next round of hangings took place on April 21, 1876. This time five men ascended the scaffold. The crime for which Orpheus McGee paid with his life was the slaying of Robert Alexander, allegedly to avenge a friend whom Alexander had killed. William Leach was convicted of murdering an itinerant minstrel. Gibson Ishtanubbee was found guilty of killing "Squirrel" Funny, a white farmer, with an ax. Isham Seely, Ishtanubbee's confederate, was convicted of beating Funny's black female companion to death. Aaron Wilson, a twenty-year-old black man, was convicted of killing a traveling merchant with an ax and the merchant's twelve-year-old son with a shotgun.

In sentencing Wilson, Parker delivered a particularly impassioned statement, beseeching the convicted man "not to waste a moment of time, but to at once devote yourself to the preparation of your soul to meet its God. . . . There is but one who can pardon your offense; there is a savior who can wash from your soul the stain of murder." He entreated Wilson to reflect upon the heinousness of his deeds: "Bring to your mind the mortal struggles and dying agonies of your murdered victims. Recall to your memory the face of that murdered boy." Apparently unmoved by the sentence of death, Wilson reportedly told the guards leading him back to the jail, "By God, that is nothing when you get used to it!"

The first men sentenced to hang were representative of those to follow, in terms of the motives for their crimes, racial composition, weapons used, and demeanor in the courtroom and on the scaffold. Many of them killed to rob their victims, often of paltry sums or a few items of clothing. A few made off with substantial amounts of money or valuable property, such as horses and cattle. Several took the lives of friends, business partners, wives, relatives, neighbors, or people who

The hanging of Crawford Goldsby ("Cherokee Bill"), March 17, 1896. *Archives and Manuscripts Division, Oklahoma Historical Society.*

had extended hospitality. Revenge was a factor in several of the murders, and crimes of passion also contributed to the death toll.

Some of those convicted of murder had killed lawmen sent to arrest them for lesser crimes. While Deputy Marshal William Irwin was taking Felix Griffen, the leader of a band of rustlers, to Fort Smith, two members of the gang ambushed and killed the lawman. A bounty of five hundred dollars each was announced for Jack Spaniard and Frank Palmer. Spaniard was captured, but Palmer escaped and was never heard of again in the Fort Smith court's jurisdiction. Although the prosecution was able to present only circumstantial evidence of Spaniard's guilt, it convinced the jury, which found him guilty after an hour's deliberation. Spaniard marched to the gallows on August 30, 1889. Griffen was recaptured and released on bail, but he returned to horse thievery and was eventually killed.

Alcohol was a common element in homicide and other crimes. Like William J. Whittington, other condemned men blamed their fate on the influence of drink and admonished the onlookers at the hangings to avoid the "devil's brew." Just before he was dropped through the trap in 1891, nineteen-year-old Bood Crumpton announced, "To all you who are present, especially you young men—the next time you are about to take a drink of whisky, look closely into the bottom of the glass and see if you cannot observe in there a hangman's noose. There is where I saw the one which now breaks my neck."

Others were similarly contrite; but some expressed no remorse. Defiance, self-pity, flippancy, tearful farewells, anguish, panic, religious fervor, and protestations of innocence were among the many reactions of people sentenced to death. When told by Parker that he was to hang by the neck until dead, Lewis Holder trembled, screamed, and fainted. In the jail he begged the guards not to hang him. When they ignored him, he swore that his ghost would return to haunt Parker and all others connected to the court.

Young Johnny Pointer remained cocky throughout his 1894 murder trial. The spoiled son of a well-off family from Eureka Springs, Arkansas, he had earlier had scrapes with the law in Missouri, the Indian Territory, and Arkansas. His parents managed to keep him out of jail until he was arrested for killing two traders who were traveling in the Choctaw Nation with a large bankroll. The jury found him guilty of both killings (but Parker suspended the sentence for one of them) and he appealed to the Supreme Court. The High Court had no difficulty affirming the results of the trial at Fort Smith, holding that there had been no error in Parker's instructions to the jury, his joining the two charges of murder, or the methods used in empaneling the jury. As the hour of Pointer's execution neared, his arrogance deserted him. By the time he reached the gallows, the ashen-faced Pointer's knees buckled so badly he could barely stand.

In one of the most dramatic incidents of Parker's career, Mat Music's courtroom response to his conviction for raping a six-year-old girl and infecting her with gonorrhea was to attempt to leap over Parker's head and escape by plunging through a window. The judge grabbed the defendant by the neck and wrestled him to the floor.

Entreating hapless criminals to be spiritually prepared to meet their Maker became a regular part of the judge's sentencing statements. So did the castigating of those convicted of the worst crimes. After the jury found Gus Bogles guilty of a brutal killing, Parker reminded him that he had tried to retract an earlier confession, thereby adding "to your crime that of perjury." Such duplicity, Parker thundered, "of course, is not to be wondered at. . . . It is expecting too much of wicked and depraved human nature for us to look for truth from one who has stained his hands with innocent human blood. . . . Sometimes such persons have succeeded, by their falsehoods, in deceiving juries and in cheating justice. You have not succeeded, and you stand before the bar of this court to have announced to you the sentence which the law attaches shall follow."

Among the many vicious criminals to stand trial before Parker, none was bolder than Crawford Goldsby, also known as "Cherokee Bill." Both his parents were mixtures of white, black, and Indian; his father was also part Mexican. Goldsby was a member of the infamous outlaw band led by Bill Cook that rampaged through the Cherokee and Creek nations in the 1890s, robbing trains, stagecoaches, a bank, stores, and travelers, and in the process killing several innocent people. Estimates of the number Goldsby killed range from seven to thirteen. The gang's activities came to the attention of the attorney general and the secretary of the interior. Demands for the gang's capture and punishment mounted, and reward notices were posted. Indian law officers, Texas Rangers, and Fort Smith deputy marshals succeeded in apprehending most of its members and bringing them before Parker. They received long prison terms for robbery. Cook himself was taken in New Mexico and hauled to Fort Smith. Parker handed down a sentence of forty-five years at the Detroit House of Correction, where he had sent the other gang members.

Of all the members of the Cook gang, only Goldsby had enough evidence against him to be charged with murder. But he remained at large and difficult to capture until a combination of subterfuge and courage eventually brought about his arrest and transport to Fort Smith. Goldsby was indicted and quickly convicted for killing a prominent citizen, Ernest Melton, during the gang's robbing of a store. Parker's fifteen-minute charge to the jury was uncharacteristically brief, and the jury returned a verdict of guilty after deliberating for only twenty minutes. The judge's sentencing statement reflected his own outrage and that of the people of the Indian Territory: "[T]here can be no doubt of your guilt. [The] evidence shows a killing of the most brutal and wicked character. . . . Melton was the innocent, unoffending victim of the savage brutality which prompted the robbery and murder." Parker said he knew this was but one of many crimes Goldsby had committed, including other murders. The "murderous act" of killing Melton "was of the most wanton and reckless character,

showing total disregard of human life." After more such stern
lecturing, Parker expressed satisfaction that all of the Cook
gang were in prison or dead. Before handing down the sentence of death, he gave his usual warning to the prisoner to
prepare his soul for the afterlife and God's final judgment.

Rather than reflect on his wicked ways and the impending
confrontation with the Almighty, Goldsby preferred to think
of a way out of his earthly predicament. His attorneys
appealed the case to the Supreme Court, and Parker accordingly issued a stay of execution. Goldsby, apparently lacking
faith in a favorable outcome from the appeal, began hatching
escape plans with other inmates on the lower level of the new
prison, known as "Murderers Row".

Guards discovered the .45 revolver and ammunition
Goldsby had persuaded a trusty to smuggle into his cell in a
bucket of lime. They failed, however, to detect a second
smuggled revolver that Goldsby had concealed behind a
brick. As guard Lawrence Keating and turnkey Campbell Eoff
were making their nightly check on the prisoners in the two
rows of the lower level, Goldsby, with the barrel of his
weapon, managed to block the locking bar that secured all
the cells on his row. He and others leaped from their cells,
and before Keating could draw his revolver, Goldsby shot him
twice, killing him. As Goldsby and prisoner George Pearce
were running for freedom, other guards appeared, along with
head jailer John D. Berry. Marshal George J. Crump arrived
and took charge. A furious gun battle ensued. The other prisoners who had planned to join the attempted breakout
thought better of it and stayed in their cells. Henry Starr, an
inmate awaiting his own trial for murder, persuaded Goldsby
that his situation was hopeless, and Cherokee Bill surren-
dered. Meanwhile, a large number of citizens had gathered
outside the jail, and when they learned of the well-regarded
Keating's death, they demanded that Goldsby be lynched.
The officers and District Attorney James F. Read succeeded
in discouraging further such talk, dispersed the crowd, and
returned the would-be escapee to his cell.

To the grand jury that was to consider this and other cases, Parker said: "I want you to return indictments in every case wherein it is probable that a murder has been committed, and first I want you to take up the case of Crawford Goldsby, alias Cherokee Bill." Goldsby's sentence for the "foul murder" of Ernest Melton, he informed the jury, had been set aside pending appeal to the Supreme Court. He now stood accused of killing Keating. "I want you to especially give that case your attention, and if you think an indictment should be returned, do so speedily, that he may be put on trial to answer for his crime." The grand jury responded with a quick indictment. At his trial Goldsby pleaded not guilty. His attorneys claimed that the court lacked jurisdiction to try the case and that their client could not get a fair trial in Fort Smith because of Keating's popularity there, but Parker angrily rejected both assertions. Assistant District Attorney J. B. McDonough's prosecution of the case was earnest and eloquent. After a three-day trial, the jury took fifteen minutes to return a guilty verdict. Again there was an appeal to the Supreme Court; again the appeal was rejected, this time on the motion of the solicitor general, because there had been "[n]o appearance for plaintiff in error." President Cleveland rejected Goldsby's application for clemency, and Parker set March 17, 1896, as the date of execution. The hanging, witnessed by the condemned man's mother and sister, took place as scheduled. Cherokee Bill had the distinction of being the only man convicted in Parker's court of a murder committed in Arkansas: the jail, being federal property, was within the district court's jurisdiction. The following month, on April 30, 1896, three condemned murderers were marched to the scaffold: George Pearce (Goldsby's fellow conspirator in the escape attempt), his brother John, and Webber Isaacs.

The next hangings, and the last of the multiple executions, were of Rufus Buck and the four other members of his gang. Their crime spree in the Creek Nation was brief—a mere thirteen days in the summer of 1895—but their actions were even more revolting than those of the Cook gang, Cherokee

Bill, or any other Indian Territory outlaws. The leader, Rufus Buck, was a Euchee Indian. Sam Sampson and Maoma July were Creeks; Lucky and Lewis Davis were mixed black and Creek. All had appeared before Parker previously for minor offenses and all had served time in the Fort Smith jail. Their crime spree began with the killing, supposedly by Buck, of a black deputy marshal, John Garrett. Next, four of them raped a woman who was moving from one farm to another with her fourteen-year-old son. Near Okmulgee they robbed a man of his horse, saddle, money, and gold watch, but decided not to kill him. Near Sapulpa they attempted to steal the horses of Gus Chambers, and when Chambers fought back, the desperadoes shot up his house. Their next victims were a stockman, whom they robbed of his clothing and boots, and a black youth traveling with him, whom they seriously wounded. They committed their final outrages at the home of Henry Hassan. They forced Hassan's wife, Rosetta, to prepare a meal, and after eating, they brutally assaulted her. They then forced her husband and a hired hand to fight each other, and while they fought, the gang members fired at their feet. Moving on, they robbed a nearby store.

News of the Buck gang's evil deeds spread quickly through the Creek Nation. A large posse of deputy marshals, Indian lighthorsemen, and Creek citizens tracked them down and, after a lengthy gun battle, forced the gang to surrender. To prevent the criminals from being lynched by the angry crowd that had assembled, the lawmen spirited them away in the dark and managed to get Buck and his confederates to Fort Smith. The grand jury indicted all five for the rape of Rosetta Hassan and for the killing of Deputy Marshal Garrett. Arraigned before Parker, they all entered not-guilty pleas. The trial on the rape charge, which began September 20, 1896, received extensive newspaper coverage.

Both of the Hassans gave heart-rending testimony. At one point Rosetta found it difficult to continue her statement, and Parker gently urged her to continue: "Just go on and tell everything that occurred there. The law makes it necessary to tell it. It is a very delicate matter, of course, but you will have to tell about it." The judge and jury, as well as the crowd in courtroom, were visibly moved by her account of the horrors she had endured.

Assistant District Attorney McDonough mounted a vigorous prosecution. His closing remarks were terse: "Gentlemen: You have heard the evidence. It was so plain it is unnecessary to argue the case. The court will give you all necessary instruction, and we will expect a verdict of guilty at your hands." The five attorneys appointed to defend the accused Buck gang did almost nothing in behalf of their clients. After short but pointed instructions by Parker, the jury retired. Without even bothering to ballot, they returned to the courtroom with a verdict of guilty. A new jury was then selected, which quickly found the prisoners guilty of murdering John Garrett.

Parker commanded the prisoners to stand, and he pronounced the sentence of death on all five. Rape, he said, was a "crime offensive to decency, and as a brutal attack upon the honor and chastity of the weaker sex." Congress had made rape a capital offense because it had been "deemed equal in enormity and wickedness to murder." The prisoners had been found guilty "of one of the most brutal, wicked, repulsive and dastardly crimes known in the annals of crime." As usual, he implored the condemned men to seek God's forgiveness: "We are taught that His mercy will wipe out even this horrible crime." But to receive God's mercy it was necessary "to make atonement for the revolting crime against His law and against human law you have committed." The prisoners heard the judge's words without visible displays of emotion. Parker issued a stay of execution pending appeals to the Supreme Court, but because no attorney appeared to present briefs on their behalf, the Court affirmed the judgments of the lower court without opinion. Apparently there was no sentence handed down for the murder of Garrett; none was needed. On July 1, 1896, Buck, Sampson, July, and the Davises dropped through the trap with broken necks.

Rufus Buck, unlike Crawford Goldsby, had reflected on the afterlife while awaiting death. In his cell was found a photograph of his mother, on the back of which he had written a poem entitled "MY, dream,—1896." Replete with eccentric punctuation and capitalization, it told of his vision of heaven and his tender thoughts of his wife, mother, and sisters. He had closed with:

<pre>
                    H
                    O
                    L
                    Y
        FATHer   Son
                    g
                    H
                    O
                    S
                    T
           virtue & resurresur.rection.
     RememBer, Me, ROCK, OF, Ages:
</pre>

The seventy-ninth and last man to be hanged as a result of a trial in Parker's court was James C. Casharego, alias George W. Wilson. He was convicted of killing and robbing a traveling companion, Zachariah W. Thatch, in the Creek Nation. Like many who committed homicide in the Indian Territory, he threw his victim into a creek. The body was discovered downstream where it had washed up. Several people testified that they had seen the two men camping on the night of the killing and that they had heard shots. In a preliminary hearing before a United States commissioner, Casharego made incriminating admissions.

Deputy marshals located the spot where the two men had camped and noticed that, to cover up the crime, a fire had been set where the victim had bled to death. At first the deputies saw no blood on the surface; dry weather had caused the ground to crack, and the blood had flowed down the crevices. They dug up several samples of earth that contained blood, which were introduced at Casharego's trial. This, along with Casharego's statement before the commissioner and other evidence, convinced the jury of his guilt. In sentencing him to the gallows, Parker told the condemned man that: "Even nature revolted against your crime; the earth opened and drank up the blood, held it in a fast embrace until the time it should appear against you; the water, too, threw up its dead and bore upon its placid bosom the foul evidence of your crime." In vain, Casharego appealed to the Supreme Court. The main point of the appeal was the admissibility at the trial of the remarks he had made to the United States commissioner. Chief Justice Melville W. Fuller concluded that the statement was admissible as evidence because it had been made voluntarily. Moreover, the commissioner had not been obliged to tell the defendant that it could be used against him or that he had a right to an attorney. Casharego was hanged on July 30, 1896.

Casharego, like most of the people Parker sentenced to death, was white, but several blacks and Indians were also hanged during his twenty-one year tenure. In 1995 a Texas congresswoman, Eddie Bernice Johnson, objected to naming a new federal building in Fort Smith in honor of Isaac Parker because "he was a racist and hung blacks just because they were black."

The charge will not hold up. There is nothing written about or by Parker to suggest that he had any animus toward nonwhites. In fact, as a congressman whose Republicanism had been molded by the Civil War and Reconstruction, he had consistently voted for measures to extend and protect the rights of black Americans. One of the reasons he welcomed the appointment of D. P. Upham as marshal was Upham's reputation as a determined foe of the Ku Klux Klan. Some of the Fort Smith court's most valued deputy marshals were black; the most notable example was Bass Reeves. Appointed in 1875, Reeves was the first black United States deputy marshal west of the Mississippi. There were at least nineteen black

deputies of Parker's court, including Bynum Colbert, Robert
Fortune, John Garrett, Grant Johnson, and Zeke Miller.
Parker's personal bailiff was George Winston, a former slave.

Parker found no pleasure in ordering the execution of anyone, black, white, or Indian. Those he sent to the scaffold
were hanged because juries had found them guilty of capital
crimes; Parker had no option but to impose the death penalty. Of the 87 men he and his predecessors on the Fort Smith
bench sentenced to death, 18 (21%) were black, 33 (38%)
were white, and 36 (41%) were Indian.

On the other hand, the men who served on the juries in the
Western District of Arkansas were white southerners.
Elsewhere in the South in that era, it was practically impossible to convict white persons for killing blacks. In Parker's
court, things were different—juries returned guilty verdicts
for whites and Indians accused of murdering blacks.

As noted above, one of the first men to be hanged after
Parker became district judge was Isham Seely, an Indian who
had bludgeoned a black woman to death. That no other people were hanged for killing blacks is the result of Supreme
Court actions. At the trial of Ely Lucas, a Choctaw accused of
killing a black man, Parker told the jury that his court had
jurisdiction in the case because the defendant was an Indian
and the victim was black. The Supreme Court ruled that it
was not up to the judge to decide citizenship. This was a
question of fact, wrote Justice George Shiras, and it was the
prosecutor's responsibility to convince the jury that the murdered black man was not a citizen of an Indian nation. The
Supreme Court remanded the case with instructions to set
aside the verdict and grant a new trial. Eventually Lucas was
tried in a Choctaw court.

John Boyd, a white, and Eugene Standley, a Choctaw,
stood trial for killing a black, John Dansby. In submitting the
case to the jury, Parker stated that it was "one of great mag-
nitude, great importance. I ask you to do that equal and exact
justice that you are commanded by the oath you have
assumed." The jury returned verdicts of guilty, and Parker

sentenced the two men to hang. The Supreme Court, speaking through John Marshall Harlan, reversed the judgment on the grounds that Parker should not have allowed the prosecution to present evidence that the defendants had committed robberies. "However depraved in character, and however full of crime their past lives may have been, the defendants were entitled to be tried upon competent evidence, and only for the offence charged." Retried at Fort Smith, Boyd and Standley were found guilty of manslaughter and sentenced to ten years' imprisonment.

In another case, Charles Smith, a white man, was tried and convicted for the murder of John Welch, a black man. Again the Supreme Court reversed the judgment. In an opinion delivered by Justice Horace Gray, the Court held that Parker had erred in telling the jury that the witnesses for the defendant, who had described Welch as a "quarrelsome and dangerous man," were not of good character. "[S]ee to it," Parker had instructed the jury, "that [the verdict] is the reflection not by keepers of dives and gambling hells, and violators of law, and prison convicts." Such testimony, said Parker, must be "cast aside as so much worthless matter invoked wrongfully." The Supreme Court objected to this "heaping up of injurious epithets," which "could not have been understood by the jury otherwise than as a command to disregard all the testimony introduced in behalf of the defendant." The Court remanded the case, with directions to set aside the verdict, and ordered a new trial. Smith's second trial ended with a manslaughter conviction and a ten-year sentence.

The trial of Robert M. Hall perhaps reflects Parker's views about trials elsewhere in the South in which whites stood accused of killing blacks. Hall was white, as was the man he was charged with murdering. The district attorney remarked that the defendant had killed a black man in Mississippi but had been acquitted. Such trials there, he said, were "farces." Parker overruled the defense counsel's objection to the statement and held that the court could take judicial note "of the fact or supposed fact that trials of white men in Mississippi for killing negroes are farces, and that counsel could properly allude to any historical fact or facts 'generally recognized by everybody.'"

The jury returned a verdict of guilty, and Hall appealed. The Supreme Court again handed down a reversal. Speaking for his brethren, Justice Gray found that the district attorney's argument "was evidently calculated and intended to persuade the jury that the defendant had murdered one man in Mississippi, and should therefore be convicted of murdering another man in Arkansas." The district attorney's conduct "was a breach of professional and official duty, which, upon the defendant's protest, should have been rebuked by the court, and the jury directed to allow it no weight." Parker's failure to so instruct the jury amounted to "a grave error, manifestly tending to prejudice the defendant with the jury." Hall was acquitted on retrial at Fort Smith.

Of the 344 people brought before Parker for capital offenses, the great majority were men. Only a handful of women were charged with capital offenses, and none was executed. There was great reluctance—on the part of presidents, attorneys general, Fort Smith juries, the public, and even Parker, the prosecuting attorneys, and executioner George Maledon— to have a woman hang. The first woman tried for murder in Parker's court was Elizabeth Owens. She and her husband were accused of killing a neighbor over a dispute about cattle. After deliberating for an hour, the jury returned a verdict of not guilty, which the courtroom spectators applauded.

In those cases where female defendants were found guilty of murder, all succeeded in having their sentences commuted to imprisonment. Twenty-year-old Fanny Echols shot and killed the man with whom she lived. Her claim that he had beaten her did not sway the jury, and Parker sentenced her to the gallows. She was to be hanged along with five men on July 11, 1884, but Parker, District Attorney Clayton, many citizens of the Creek Nation, and the jury that had convicted her implored President Chester A. Arthur to commute the sentence to life imprisonment. Believing that the request was based on sympathy for Echols as a woman, the attorney general recommended against clemency. Parker then wrote directly to President Arthur, urging commutation. A telegram of July 3, 1884, announced that the president had commuted her sentence to life. George Maledon expressed relief. He was similarly relieved when other women convicted of murder were spared the noose. Elsie James, an Indian woman convicted of killing a man with a hominy pestle, also received a commutation to life. The Supreme Court, in 1897, reversed the murder conviction of Mary A. Kettenring "upon confession of error" by the federal prosecutor. A new trial ended in acquittal.

Mollie King, a black woman, was not so fortunate. On appeal, she, too, secured a reversal from the Supreme Court based on the prosecutor's confession of error, and the court remanded the case for retrial. In the meantime, Parker died and the law was changed to allow juries the option of imposing either the death penalty or life imprisonment at hard labor for murder or rape convictions. On retrial, Mollie King was again convicted but was given a life sentence. Her gender was no doubt a factor in the court's choice of this alternative.

Parker's juries were frequently charged with determining which form of homicide the accused had committed: murder, which meant the death penalty, or homicide, which meant a prison term. The judge instructed the jurors on the legal distinctions between the two crimes. Murder, he told them, was the taking of human life willfully and with malice aforethought; that is, intentionally, without provocation or mitigating circumstances. "It is not necessary," he would tell jurors, "to show that a man had special spite or hatred or ill will against the man whom he may have killed." Another way of defining "malice aforethought" was the "killing of a human being done in such a way as to show that he who did it had a heart void of social duty and a mind fatally bent upon mischief." He commented at length on evidence, credibility of witnesses, motive, presumption of guilt, and reasonable doubt.

Manslaughter, he explained to jurymen, was "the killing of a man unlawfully and wilfully, but without malice afore-thought." It was the unlawful slaying of another person "on sudden quarrel or in the heat of passion." The victim had to provoke the killing, but words alone were not "sufficient provocation." There had to be a wrongful act committed by the victim that would create a state of passion in the mind of the person doing the killing. Passion alone, he said, did not justify the taking of a life; it had to be "hasty" passion that rendered the perpetrator "incapable of deliberating." Putting it another way, Parker said that manslaughter occupied "a midway position" between self-defense and murder. When the judge believed that a defendant was guilty of murder but the jury found instead for manslaughter, Parker let the jurors know he was displeased.

Parker's charges to juries in homicide cases tended to be lengthy, detailed, and interspersed with long quotations from legal authorities. They were so protracted that they had the potential to produce as much confusion as clarification. As will be seen, his prolix explanations of the differences between murder and manslaughter brought him into conflict with the Supreme Court.

Closely related to the question of murder versus manslaughter was the debate over the "duty to retreat." In English common law, a person being murderously assaulted could not strike back unless retreat or escape was impossible. Otherwise there was no right "to stand one's ground" and kill in self-defense. Only when one's back was to the wall could there be "excusable homicide," for which there was no penalty. The duty to retreat was considered a mark of a civi-lized society. It kept fatal encounters in Britain to a minimum.

In the colonial era and for some years thereafter, American courts continued to follow this rule. But after the Revolution there was a shift in favor of "no duty to retreat." According to historian Richard Maxwell Brown, the transformation was the product of eastern legal authorities and western judges. It was not until 1921, in the case of *Brown* v. *United States*, that the Supreme Court emphatically endorsed the rule of no duty to retreat. Long before that, however, state courts had been adopting the newer view. By the latter part of the nineteenth century, it was widely held in American tribunals that retreat was cowardly and that a "true man" had the right to stand his ground and was "not obliged to fly."

Some American legal authorities, notably Joseph H. Beale, continued to believe that "no duty to retreat" was a "brutal doctrine." It was suited only to "the ethics of the duelist, the German officer, and the buccaneer." However, by the close of the nineteenth century, a growing number of judges were proclaiming that the obligation to retreat was "contrary to the tendency of the American mind." Courts in the West and South were especially receptive to "no duty to retreat," with the courts and penal code of Texas leading the way.

Parker's court, with its Indian Territory and Arkansas jurisdiction, was both western *and* southern, but throughout his judicial career, Parker continued to adhere to the older rule of law regarding the duty to retreat. He apparently believed that acceptance of the new interpretation would encourage killings in his bailiwick, an area notorious for rampant bloodletting. His strong stand in support of the duty to retreat increasingly set him apart from other jurists of the late nineteenth century and created another area of disagreement between him and the Supreme Court.

Until appeals to the Supreme Court were allowed, a condemned person had only two hopes of obtaining a more favorable result: a motion for a new trial, or executive clemency, which had to come from the president of the United States. Executive clemency was especially important in the years before Congress authorized appeals from Parker's court. Most of the eighty-one men and women spared from hanging at Fort Smith were beneficiaries of clemency as exercised by every president from Grant to Taft (except James A. Garfield, who served only briefly). The majority of the convicted murderers and rapists so spared received a commutation to life imprisonment; some sentences were reduced even further.

The procedure for seeking executive clemency was for the person convicted to send an application for commutation or pardon to the Department of Justice. There the pardon attorney scrutinized the application and, if he thought it had merit, passed it on to the attorney general. The final determination for or against clemency rested with the president, who usually followed the attorney general's recommendation. Grover Cleveland was inclined to base his conclusions on his own careful examination of the applications and supporting papers. He was perhaps more sensitive than other presidents to such matters because, in his earlier capacity of sheriff of Erie County, New York, he had hanged two men, a duty required of him by law and that he had found repugnant.

The granting of executive clemency was usually in response to appeals from attorneys for the prisoners, supported by letters from their families and friends, respected citizens, prison officials, and the attorney general. Surprisingly, many applications received support from the district attorneys who had prosecuted the condemned men and jurors who had helped convict them. Parker himself recommended clemency in a number of instances. Among the many justifications for clemency Parker and the others advanced were insufficient evidence of malice, premeditation, or intent to kill; conviction based on circumstantial evidence; youth of the convict; insanity; mitigating circumstances; "doubt as to guilt"; conflicting testimony; circumstances that developed after a conviction; "great provocation"; "not a case for the death penalty"; "in consideration of all the circumstances and the long confinement already suffered"; "statement of the district attorney that the crime was manslaughter"; and failing health and little likelihood of living much longer. Three men received commutation to life imprisonment because their offenses were committed "during a factional war in the Creek Nation." Good conduct while in prison was sometimes a factor in the granting of a pardon or a shortened sentence. People convicted of murder or rape whose sentences were commuted after Parker's intercession included, among others, William

Alexander, John Broderick, Fannie Echols, Sahquahnee (a Sac and Fox Indian), Oscar Snow, and Edward Wilkey.

A number of condemned men even gained pardons. One was Mat Music, whose attempted escape Parker had thwarted. As it turned out, his desperate bid for freedom was unnecessary. He was convicted in 1883 and scheduled to hang the following year, but doubts as to his guilt were evident at the trial. The six-year-old supposed rape victim was probably too young to give creditable testimony, there was evidence that the girl's mother had coached her on what to say at the trial, and her "gonorrhea" may have been an inflammation of the genitalia caused by a long horseback ride. Parker and District Attorney Clayton recommended that the death sentence be commuted to life imprisonment. President Arthur went a step further. He found it "extremely doubtful whether [Music] was guilty of the crime wherewith he is charged" and granted a full pardon. Earlier, President Grant commuted Charles Thomas's 1876 sentence to life at the Moundsville, West Virginia, prison because there had been "great provocation" for the homicide for which he had been convicted. President Rutherford B. Hayes later issued Thomas a pardon because Judge Parker "earnestly recommended" it in a telegram to him.

In another case, Meredith Crow's murder conviction in 1885 was commuted to life; President Grover Cleveland pardoned him after nine years at the Detroit House of Correction. The president remarked that, "If the recommendations of the judge and district attorney or the advice of the Attorney-General had been followed in the terms of the last commutation, the prisoner would have before this time been discharged." William J. Meadows, whose sentence had earlier been commuted to life on Parker's recommendation, received a pardon, which Parker and the district attorney supported, after sixteen years' imprisonment. In still another case, Parker and the district attorney encouraged George Brashears's successful appeal for clemency because they believed the evidence indicated manslaughter, not the murder finding of the jury.

President Cleveland also granted a pardon to Blue Duck, a Cherokee whose main claim to fame was having posed for a photograph with the notorious Belle Starr. Benjamin Harrison had earlier commuted his 1886 death sentence to life imprisonment at the Menard, Illinois, facility because there was "some doubt as to his guilt." Blue Duck was pardoned in 1895 because he was dying of tuberculosis and presumably would not live more than a month after release; therefore he would be allowed "to die among his friends" in the Indian Territory.

Sometimes a prisoner's mental condition was a factor in the granting of clemency. In one instance, Parker and the district attorney "earnestly recommended" the commutation of John Jacobs's murder conviction because he was an "Indian and of such a low order of intelligence as to lessen his degree of guilt." Jacobs had "acted under a mistaken idea of his right to slay, and . . . lacks sufficient mental and moral responsibility to warrant his being punished by death." Occasionally, the awarding of clemency was based on self-defense, as in the case of William Dickson. The attorney general, district attorney, and Parker endorsed Dickson's successful appeal for the commutation of his death sentence to life imprisonment "upon the theory that there was a strong likelihood that the person killed stood ready to kill [Dickson] if he was quick enough."

Parker frequently recommended against clemency. One example is his reaction to the attempt of Patrick McCarty to receive a commutation. McCarty had killed and robbed his traveling companions, two brothers named Mahoney, in the Cherokee Nation. When arrested, McCarty confessed to the murders; he was tried before Parker, convicted, and sentenced to hang. His attorneys petitioned President Cleveland for clemency, but Parker wrote a long, forceful statement against granting it, citing several facts brought out in the testimony at trial. Cleveland accordingly refused to intercede, and McCarty went to the gallows on April 8, 1887.

In only two instances did convicted murderers, both black, receive clemency against Parker's express wishes. Several prominent citizens went over Parker's head and urged clemency for Irving Perkins, who had been convicted of poisoning the baby he had fathered with his stepdaughter. President Hayes commuted the sentence to life at hard labor. Also bypassing Parker were those who sought clemency for Carolina Grayson. Grayson, along with his brother Peter, Manuel Lewis, and Robert Love, was sentenced to death for murdering a man whom they believed had stolen hogs. Based on the recommendations of Parker and District Attorney Clayton, the sentences of Peter Grayson, Lewis, and Love were commuted to life at hard labor. Petitioners, many of them black, took the case of Carolina Grayson directly to President Hayes, who again responded with a commutation to life. Years later, Love secured his release based on the dying confession of the "real murderer."

In both instances, Parker was furious that his recommendations against clemency were ignored. He became increasingly exasperated with attorneys who routinely petitioned the presidents for pardons or commutations. Particularly offensive to him was Thomas Marcum, whom he denounced as a "pardon broker" and a "drunken lawyer" who conducted his practice in the saloons of Fort Smith.

Historian Jeffrey Burton has suggested that it was well that the law permitted those whom Parker had sentenced to hang to petition for clemency. In Burton's view, the officials in Washington responsible for acting on the petitions were in a position to respond objectively: they were relatively unfamiliar with the state of affairs in the Indian Territory, not influenced by courtroom passions and oratory, and unaffected by the immediate force of Parker's personality.

History, of course, remembers Parker for the hangings he ordered, not for his role in executive clemency. In his own time, the judge's national notoriety came in large part from comparisons of his record of death sentences with those of other American courts. The United States District Court for the Eastern District of Texas, as will be seen, acquired jurisdiction over a large part of the Indian Territory in 1889. In the following three years, of 169 persons charged with murder, 108 were indicted; of these, just one was convicted of murder and eight were convicted of manslaughter. No one was executed until 1894. Texas juries were well known for their willingness to find mitigating circumstances such as self-defense. In comparison with Fort Smith juries, the Texans were also less likely to find defendants guilty in noncapital cases.

In the period from 1890 to 1892, there were 16,987 murders reported nationwide. From this number came 332 executions and 557 lynchings. But only three lynchings took place in Parker's jurisdiction during the twenty-one years that he sat on the federal bench. In an 1892 charge to a grand jury he exclaimed: "Great God, what a picture! What is the matter with the system of jurisprudence in this country that more men each year are taken out by the violence of the mob, by the fury of the populace and put to death?" The lynchings were themselves murders "of the most brutal and horrible character and they may be added to the grand total of the other murderers." He told another grand jury in 1895 that mob violence and lynch law were to be found in areas where the citizens had no confidence in their courts. He proudly pointed out that there were "no mobs in the counties of this state which are in this jurisdiction" and that the low rate of illicit executions in the Indian Territory, "not the amount of it that you would naturally expect from the criminal condition of that country," was because people there had faith in his court.

Not surprisingly, as Parker's national reputation grew, there were those who regarded him as an ogre. The judge was well aware of the negative image of his court. To the 1895 grand jury, he said that there were those who condemned him and his juries for doing what was clearly their duty: to stem the tide of lawlessness in the Indian Territory. Lawyers who had failed to get their clients acquitted were to blame for creating a false impression of judicial tyranny: "There is where it started from; there is the origin of it. Many [attorneys] have acted

outrageously in that particular, disgracefully, unprofessional-
ly, and in every other way that ought to be reprimanded. That
is the truth about it." He acknowledged to a newspaperman
that "People have said that I am a cruel, heartless, and blood-
thirsty man." "[B]ut," he insisted, "I have ever had the single aim of justice in view. . . . Do equal and exact justice is my
motto."

CHAPTER 4

Lesser Crimes

ISAAC Parker's historical reputation rests largely on the number of people he sentenced to be hanged. Yet capital cases accounted for only a small fraction of his caseload. Of the 13,490 cases he tried, 1,155 involved murder or manslaughter. Even when 1,529 assaults and 115 other violent crimes are added, violent crime accounted for less than twenty-one percent of the total.

His crowded docket consisted mainly of a host of lesser offenses: adultery; aiding in the escape of a prisoner; arson; assault; assault with intent to kill; bigamy; bribery; conspiracy; embezzlement; extortion; forgery; fraud; gambling; illegal grazing; impeding justice; impersonating an officer; incest; intimidating a witness; introducing liquor into the Indian country; kidnapping; larceny; perjury; receiving stolen property; resisting arrest; and timber trespass.

These cases were ordinarily tried in state courts but came to Parker because of his Indian Territory jurisdiction. He also presided over trials for offenses that Congress had defined as federal crimes. In these cases, the defendants included both Arkansas and Indian Territory inhabitants. Among the federal crimes were counterfeiting; mutilating or defacing currency; breaches of the internal revenue laws; violation of the postal statutes; perjury; and violation of voting rights.

Parker's instructions to a grand jury in 1895 emphasized the gravity of these nonviolent federal offenses. Counterfeiting was "a matter that you are to look at carefully, because the circulating money of the country which passes into the pockets of the people, and which they received in exchange for the products of their toil, is required by the law to be kept entirely pure." Because of the importance the American people attached to the postal system ("we would rather do without one of our meals than to miss our mail one time"), it was necessary to enforce rigorously the laws protecting the mail. Postal crimes included sending obscene mail, obstructing the mail, and robbing the mail or a post office. "The mails paid for by the people," said Parker, "are not to be used as a conduit for crime, for the perpetuation of crimes, or for the productions of bad morals, vice and licentiousness." Although the judge praised postal authorities for zealous enforcement of the statutes affecting their department, he complained that the law did not protect human life nearly as effectively as it protected the mail.

Parker also underscored the court's interest in punishing perjury. It was the duty of all persons connected to the court to "uncover perjury, to uncover falsehood, and bring to justice false accusers or false witnesses." For Parker, perjury in his court was no doubt a personal affront as well as a violation of the law.

Another federal crime the judge brought to the attention of the grand jurors in 1895 was the violation of the liquor tax. Spirit distillers, brewers, and wholesale and retail dealers were required to pay annual taxes. Evading the tax, Parker said, not only deprived the government of revenue but was unfair to those who abided by the law and paid the tax.

The introduction of liquor into the Indian country was a crime that had plagued Indian police and federal authorities since the creation of the Indian Territory. The problem became worse as more whites flooded into the land of the Five Nations. The penalty for those found guilty in Parker's court was three months in jail and a fine of two hundred and fifty dollars. Hundreds of offenders were caught and convicted, but the punishment did not deter those who stood to profit from the illicit trade.

One notable case required Parker to interpret the laws against alcohol in the Indian Territory. The main question before the court in the case of *United States* v. *Ellis* (1892) was whether lager beer was "spirituous liquor" within the meaning of the 1832 law against introducing liquor into the Indian country, or whether the law covered only distilled beverages. After emphasizing the great damage liquor had done to the Indians, claiming that "[I]t has swept whole tribes out of existence," Parker stated that the law had been passed to prevent drunkenness among them—regardless of the form of liquor. He pointed out that fermentation, not distillation, produced alcohol. Although he acknowledged that courts had differed on the definition of spirituous liquors, he insisted that Congress had intended the statute to include beer and ale as well as distilled beverages.

Another case covering the liquor question came before Parker in 1892 with a similar result: a jury found the defendant, R. Sarlls, guilty of bringing lager beer into the Choctaw Nation. Sarlls, however, appealed the conviction to the Supreme Court, arguing that Parker had erred in refusing a request to instruct the jury that lager beer was not a spirituous liquor. A unanimous Court, speaking through Justice George Shiras, reversed the verdict and remanded the case with directions to quash the indictment and discharge the defendant. Shiras and his colleagues on the Supreme Court emphatically disagreed with Parker's interpretation. Citing dictionaries, popular usage, and the Roman historian Tacitus, as well as state and federal statutes and precedents, the Court held that beer and ale were not spirituous liquors. Justice Shiras noted, however, that soon after Sarlls's conviction in the lower court, the Intoxicants Act of 1892 had explicitly included beer, ale, and wine among the spirituous liquors that could not legally be sold in the Indian Territory. Thus Parker's view and the law were now in harmony, but since the change came after Sarlls's trial in the lower court, it could not affect his appeal. Because of the troubles—many of them fatal—attributed to the consumption of alcohol within his jurisdiction, Parker probably was tempted to stretch the law to cover fermented beverages. A Fort Smith grand jury of 1887 found that "about ninety-five percent of the criminal matters presented us are directly or indirectly traceable to intoxicants as the cause."

After the Sarlls decision and the passage of the Intoxicants Act of 1892, questions still remained about the status of "Choctaw beer," a low-alcohol beverage that white miners and other non-Indian residents of the Choctaw and Chickasaw nations favored. Parker ruled that its sale, but not its manufacture, was illegal. In fact, the Intoxicants Act of 1892 failed to prohibit the manufacturing of beer, ale, and wine. Congress remedied the situation with legislation of 1895 forbidding the manufacture as well as sale of "any vinous, malt, or fermented liquors, or any other intoxicating drinks of any kind whatever, whether medicated or not," in the Indian Territory.

Timber trespass was another crime that took up a great deal of time in Parker's court. In the 1870s and 1880s, poachers mounted an unprecedented assault on the white oak and southern pine forests of Arkansas and the Indian Territory. The most lucrative market was the spreading railway network, which needed great quantities of wood for ties, bridges, telegraph poles, snow fences, and depots. Federal legislation of 1831, 1859, and 1878 threatened fines and imprisonment for anyone found guilty of cutting, removing, or destroying trees on public lands in Arkansas. Trees on tribal lands in the Indian Territory could be cut and removed only with the permission of and payment to the Indians. In practice, the laws proved a feeble defense against the onslaught of unscrupulous whites seeking profits from the illegal taking of timber. Enforcement was inadequate, and there was no clear federal timber policy. Arkansas juries were reluctant to convict local citizens for violations. People accused of poaching often claimed that they were homesteaders or that the boundaries of the federal lands were not clearly delineated. Mill operators who purchased the illegal lumber from poachers testified that they knew nothing about stolen timber.

One writer, Bradley W. Kidder, has suggested that Parker was especially concerned about the taking of trees reserved for naval construction. Kidder points out that the judge's membership in the House Committee on Naval Appropriations in the 42d Congress had made him mindful of the needs of America's navy. In two cases in the early 1880s, Parker ruled that the timber on federal land in northwestern Arkansas was "set aside for the use of the Navy of the United States." From 1884 until the judge's death, the great majority of the cases of Arkansas timber trespass brought before him involved timber earmarked for military use.

Unfortunately, in the Five Nations, Indians often received nothing for wood taken from their lands, or they were compensated at a much lower rate than whites in neighboring states. Sometimes payment was in the form of illegal whiskey. Despite the efforts of Parker, law officers, and government prosecutors to crack down on poachers, the looting continued. As with the liquor traffic, the potential for profit remained a great temptation, and there were many repeat offenders. In Parker's time, the punishment was only a ten-dollar fine and ten days in jail.

Parker ruefully acknowledged in *United States* v. *Reese* (1879) that punishing timber trespass in the lands belonging to the Cherokee Nation was virtually impossible. The defendant, Reese, had been charged with cutting timber on tribal lands. A frustrated and angry Parker ruled that the lands in question did not belong to the United States, that Reese's act was not covered by the statutes prohibiting the cutting of timber on federal lands, and that he was therefore not subject to any penalty. Noting that "complaints of depredations upon the timber of the Indian lands are constantly being made to officers of this court," the judge denounced the "class of men on the borders of the Indian country who revel in the idea that they have an inherent, natural right to steal from the Indians. This is not to be questioned. They think it a tyrannical use of authority if they are interfered with."

Although Parker wanted to protect Indian timber lands, after his 1879 ruling, Indian law enforcement officers were reluctant to seize stolen timber. As one white explained:

"They seam [*sic*] afraid. Fort Smith is such a terror to all Indians from the lowest to the Higest [*sic*]." Parker later insisted that Congress had an obligation to protect Indian timber lands. Such legislation was needed to "teach persons that Indians have rights which should be respected." He stated emphatically that if Congress should ever enact a law prohibiting the rape of Indian timber lands, "we will lay its mailed hand upon its violators in such a way that the timber in that Indian Territory will be protected from the rapacity of those who are now stealing it."

In a similar vein, the commissioner of the General Land Office, the agency that administered unappropriated federal lands, defined the problem in his 1882 report: "Depredations upon the public timber by powerful corporations, wealthy mill owners, lumber companies and unscrupulous monopolists are still being committed to an alarming extent and great public detriment." He complained that his agency was "powerless to prevent and seemingly legally powerless to punish the extensive looting of public timber under existing regulations."

Parker found that his court also lacked the power to punish another form of encroachment on Indian lands: illegal grazing. Vast tracts of prime cattle country lay within the Cherokee Nation. The tribe permitted United States citizens to graze their herds there, but only after buying a permit. The cattlemen ignored the requirement. The Cherokees attempted to confiscate the property of the trespassers, but, in an 1877 charge to a jury, Parker announced that the Indians lacked the authority to do so: "The fact of a man being in the Indian country without a permit is no excuse for seizing his property. Neither the Indian Sheriff nor any other officers of the Indian country can seize or remove him or his property." The proper course of action, he said, was to report violations to the president of the United States, who would dispatch soldiers to eject the offenders. "The Indians are protected against intruders by a power much more potent than their own, which will vindicate their rights whenever invoked." In fact, the troops in the area were unable to provide effective enforcement, and Parker knew it.

Another group of whites who coveted the resources of the Indian Territory and added to Parker's already heavy case load were David L. Payne and his land-hungry followers. Payne, a former Kansas legislator, was a would-be Moses who sought to lead his disciples, known as "boomers," to a Promised Land in the western part of the Indian Territory. The area in question had belonged to the Five Nations, but because many members of the tribes had sided with the Confederacy, the treaties of 1866 between the federal government and the nations of the Indian Territory had taken away one-third of their lands. Some of the acreage was now assigned to Plains Indians: Arapaho, Cheyenne, Comanche, Kiowa, and tribes moved from Kansas. In the middle of the region was the Oklahoma District, which consisted of nearly two million acres. The district had not been assigned to any of the removed tribes. Payne and his boomers argued that it was part of the public domain and open to whites under the terms of the Preemption Act of 1841 and the Homestead Act of 1862.

In 1879, Payne led the first of his several colonizing expeditions into the "Unassigned Lands." Secretary of the Interior Carl Schurz rejected Payne's interpretation of the public domain status of the area and asked the army's help in preventing these incursions. The army put troops on the Kansas border, where the boomers assembled, and sometimes chased them into the Indian Territory. Schurz pointed out that the area was within the jurisdiction of the United States District Court for the Western District of Arkansas, and accordingly, the soldiers repeatedly hauled captured boomers to Fort Smith. The only legal penalty was a fine of one thousand dollars if convicted twice. Most of Payne's followers were unable to pay. They were routinely released, only to return in another of their leader's forays into the forbidden lands.

Officials in the War and Interior departments strongly recommended that laws be enacted to stipulate prison terms for the illegal colonizers. Bills to do so were introduced in Congress, but none passed. Presidents Hayes, Arthur, and Cleveland, in 1879, 1880, 1884, and 1885, issued strongly worded proclamations warning, in Hayes's words, "certain evil disposed persons" who were attempting to settle illegally in the Indian Territory "that they will be speedily and immediately removed therefrom."

Payne himself was twice arrested and convicted, which meant he was subject to a fine for the second offense. Because he was unable or unwilling to pay the thousand dollars, the government brought a civil suit in the Fort Smith court, *United States* v. *Payne* (1881), to recover the amount owed. The lands concerned in the case lay between the Canadian River and the North Fork of the Canadian, and between the 97th and 98th meridians. They had originally belonged to the Creeks, who ceded them to the Seminole Nation in 1856. The United States regained title in 1866, but because the lands had not yet been assigned to any tribe, Payne asserted that whites had the right to purchase or homestead them.

Earlier, in 1880, the International Council of the Five Civilized Tribes created a Committee of Prosecution to aid government attorneys in the suit against Payne. Parker and District Attorney Clayton requested the committee's help in interpreting the treaties and land cessions relevant to the case, and members of the committee went to Fort Smith to present their views. The Indians believed that Payne was a tool of railroad corporations who coveted the Unassigned Lands. Indeed, one of Payne's attorneys was the president of the St. Louis and San Francisco Railroad.

Parker's decision rejected Payne's arguments. Citing several legal authorities, Parker held that Congress had clearly intended that the area in controversy be reserved for the future settlement of Indian tribes and freedmen of the Five Nations. Parker found it beyond belief that the United States would own lands that were not within the jurisdiction of the federal government or any state or territory. Land with such a status "might become a place of refuge for criminals and outlaws who could depredate and prey upon their Indian neighbors and others with impunity." The government, he emphasized, "has pledged protection and security from intruders to all the tribes in the Indian country."

Payne's followers lost momentum when he died in 1884. Nevertheless, pressure to allow whites to acquire the Unassigned Lands continued, and in 1889 Congress opened the Oklahoma District to homesteaders. The following year, the Senate Judiciary Committee concluded that District Attorney Clayton and others had used their positions to acquire Oklahoma lands before they were officially opened.

Parker, the district attorneys, deputy marshals, and the army did what they could to keep whiskey peddlers, timber poachers, and land-grabbers out of the Indian Territory. Yet they found that congressional action or, more often, inaction, hindered their attempts to protect the Indians. Their efforts were also frustrated by the failure of the nation's lawmakers to provide the personnel and funding necessary for vigorous enforcement.

Parker and the law-abiding citizens of the territory thought it important to bring to justice those who sought to exploit the Indians and their resources. These matters accounted for a high percentage of his cases. Yet the trials of violators of the liquor, timber, and land laws received far less attention in the press than did cases involving sensational crimes and notorious persons. Notable examples were the appearances before him of Myra Maybelle Shirley, better known to posterity as Belle Starr. The "Bandit Queen" was regal neither in appearance nor authority. She was not a particularly accomplished bandit; her reputation as an outlaw is far out of proportion to her actual misdeeds. Her brushes with Parker's court, however, illustrate several aspects of criminality in the Indian Territory and the workings of the court.

Belle Starr's difficulties with the law were largely the result of her propensity to marry or cohabit with outlaws, rather than a criminal nature of her own. In Texas, she married her first husband, a robber named Jim Reed, but he was killed in

Belle Starr, the best known outlaw to be sentenced to prison by Parker. *Archives and Manuscripts Division, Oklahoma Historical Society.*

1874. She took up with Bruce Younger, a gambler, horse thief, and relative of the infamous Younger brothers of Missouri. Her next husband was Sam Starr, a Cherokee thief. The marriage made her a citizen of the Cherokee Nation, where the couple took up residence in a cabin near Eufaula.

In 1882, a commissioner of the court for the Western District of Arkansas issued an arrest warrant charging Sam and Belle with stealing a horse belonging to Andrew Crane, a young, crippled white man. Deputy Marshal L. W. Marks pursued and captured them. Throughout the journey to Fort Smith, according to Fannie Blythe Marks, the wife of the deputy, Belle was an "exasperating prisoner." She continued to be difficult while incarcerated, protesting that they had only borrowed the horse. They were also accused of stealing a second horse, but because it belonged to another Indian, the second charge was dropped against Sam, but not her.

Following a hearing, a grand jury indicted the Starrs "for Larceny in the Indian Country." The pair hired attorney Benjamin Du Val and the Fort Smith law firm of William M. Cravens and Thomas Marcum. During the four-day trial, the local press turned the tawdry affair into an early chapter of the Belle Starr legend. The *Fort Smith New Era* described her as "the leader of a band of horse thieves and wielding a power over them as their queen and guiding spirit." Such coverage filled the courtroom with spectators.

During the trial, Belle dashed off several notes to her attorneys and "tried to stare down Judge Parker." She also made it apparent that she was furious with District Attorney Clayton for ridiculing Sam's illiteracy. Du Val argued that the court lacked jurisdiction because Belle was an Indian by virtue of her marriage to Sam and that the victim, Crane, was "of Indian blood and probably a citizen of the Cherokee Nation." Clayton disputed this assertion and Parker agreed with him, ruling that the cases belonged in his court. Other ploys offered by the defense also failed. Unintimidated by Belle's fierce demeanor, the jury found her guilty of stealing two horses, and Sam guilty of stealing one. Parker sentenced her to two six-month terms of imprisonment; Sam received a sentence of one year. Perhaps Belle received a lighter punishment because she was a woman.

The Starrs, along with nineteen other prisoners and five guards, boarded the prison railroad car, "Old Ten Spot," in which they began their journey to the Detroit House of Correction. No doubt the institution's reputation as a model prison influenced Parker's decision to send the Starrs there. Before leaving, Belle wrote to her daughter, Pearl, assuring her that she was not going to be "shut up in a gloomy prison"; rather, the Detroit House of Correction was "said to be one of the finest institutions in the United States, surrounded by beautiful grounds, with fountains and everything nice." Belle apparently took advantage of the programs offered and was given only light work to perform. Sam did hard labor. Both were released for good behavior after nine months.

In 1886, Belle was again in trouble with the law. An alleged murderer living with the Starrs, John Middleton, had fled on a one-eyed mare that Belle was accused of having stolen. She went voluntarily to Fort Smith and turned herself in to the marshal. Parker set a trial date and released her after she posted bond. Later in 1886, Belle was again in Fort Smith, this time accused of leading a gang in a robbery. Pleading not guilty, she requested witnesses, posted bond, and reveled in her notoriety, which by now was national. She posed for two photographs. In one, in which Deputy Marshal Tyner Hughes also appears, she sits sidesaddle on a horse, holding a riding whip and a borrowed pistol. The other shows her with a hand on the shoulder of the convicted Cherokee murderer, Blue Duck. At the commissioner's hearing, where she was again represented by the law firm of Cravens and Marcum, witnesses for the prosecution were unable to identify her positively, and she was discharged.

Returning to her Indian Territory home, Belle convinced her husband to go voluntarily to Fort Smith to face a post office burglary charge. After he was indicted, she posted a bond and secured his release. The couple lingered in Fort

Smith to take in the Seventh Annual Fair of Western Arkansas
and the Indian Territory. As part of a "wild west" entertain-
ment, she impressed the locals with feats of riding and shooting. The tale of her participation in a mock stagecoach robbery, with Judge Parker as a passenger, is apparently a product of *Hell on the Border* author Samuel W. Harman's imagination. While in Fort Smith, she made an unsuccessful effort
to prevent the conviction of her father-in-law, Tom Starr, for
"liquor and stock violations." Parker sent Tom to the Ohio
State Penitentiary in Columbus.

Soon after their return to the Cherokee Nation, Sam was
killed at a dance. Belle's next consort was another Cherokee,
Bill July, alias James July Starr. In 1889 he went to Fort Smith
to answer a charge of horse stealing. Belle was later gunned
down in the Indian Territory by an unknown assailant.
Although there were a number of suspects, no one was
brought to trial for her killing.

One of those under suspicion was her son, James Edwin
"Eddie" Reed, whom Parker sentenced to five years in the
penitentiary in Columbus for horse theft and another two
years for receiving stolen goods. In 1894 President Cleveland
pardoned Eddie at the expiration of his five-year sentence so
that his rights of citizenship could be restored. Soon after his
release, he was back in Fort Smith, this time to face
Commissioner Wheeler on a charge of introducing liquor
into the Indian country. The matter was dropped for lack of
evidence. In an odd turn of events, Eddie became a deputy
marshal for the Western District of Arkansas and proved to be
a proficient officer. He was killed while attempting to arrest
two whiskey sellers in 1896.

Belle's daughter, Pearl, had hired the attorneys who
secured her brother Eddie's 1894 pardon. In the course of
plying her trade as a prostitute, and later a madam, in Fort
Smith and elsewhere, Pearl often ran afoul of the law. Since
her transgressions were not of a federal nature, she was one
member of the Starr family who was never a defendant in
Parker's court.

The federal court at Fort Smith was under attack almost from its beginning. Congress continually attempted to reduce or eliminate the court's Indian Territory jurisdiction or to abolish the court altogether. At the same time, many bills to do away with the tribal courts were introduced. These moves were usually linked with attempts to eliminate Indian self-government, diminish the influence of the federal courts, and prepare the Indian Territory for statehood by giving it the traditional forms of American territorial government. Some leaders of the Five Nations favored territorial status; others saw the move as an assault on their sovereignty and as paving the way for white dominance. A growing animosity toward Parker and what were seen as his cruel and high-handed ways spurred Congress to demand change. Also, some in Congress believed that the Fort Smith court, with its vast area and large corps of deputy marshals, was too expensive to operate.

As a result, in 1883, Congress took away the court's jurisdiction over the northern, southern, and western portions of the Indian Territory. The legislation gave the Wichita division of the Kansas federal court jurisdiction over "all that part of the Indian Territory lying north of the Canadian river and east of Texas and the one hundredth meridian not set apart and occupied by the Cherokee, Creek, and Seminole Indian tribes," and the Quapaw Agency, which occupied the tiny corner of northeastern Indian Territory. The act also extended the jurisdiction of the District Court for the Northern District of Texas, at Graham, over the remainder of the Indian Territory lying outside of the lands of the Five Nations (present-day southwestern Oklahoma). An act of 1889 further limited the geographical extent of the Fort Smith court by taking away its jurisdiction over the Chickasaw Nation and most of the Choctaw Nation and giving it to the new federal district court for the Eastern District of Texas, at Paris. Most of the population of Indian Territory—and most of its criminal activity—was still within the domain of the Fort Smith tribunal.

Of all those who sought to limit or abolish the court for the Western District of Arkansas, no one was more persistent and

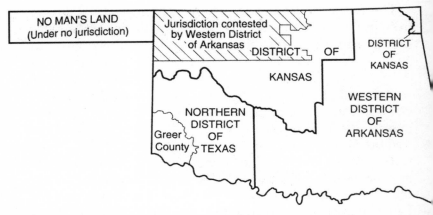

Federal Judicial Districts of Indian Territory, January 6, 1883 to Februar
28, 1889. Reproduced from Jeffrey Burton, *Indian Territory and th
United States, 1866–1906: Courts, Government, and the Movement fo
Oklahoma Statehood* (Norman: University of Oklahoma Press, 1995, 121)

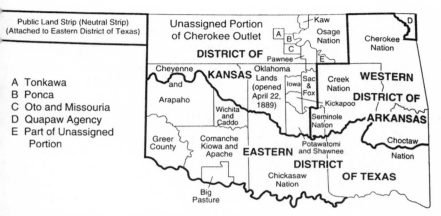

Federal Judicial Districts of Indian Territory, March 1, 1889 to May 1, 1890. Reproduced from Jeffrey Burton, *Indian Territory and the United States, 1866–1906: Courts, Government, and the Movement for Oklahoma Statehood* (Norman: University of Oklahoma Press, 1995, 152).

vituperative than Parker's nemesis, Senator George G. Vest of
Missouri. A Democrat and former Confederate soldier, Vest's
feelings about Parker may have dated from the judge's earlier days as a fellow political figure in Missouri. As historian
Jeffrey Burton has written, Vest's hostility toward Parker and
his court was "so violent that it is impossible not to conclude
that he cherished a deep and personal loathing" for the jurist
at Fort Smith. Vest denounced Parker's court as "a slaughter
house." He accused its deputy marshals, quite unfairly, of
"hunting up petty offenders in order to get the costs" rather
than to go after the true desperadoes and meet them "pistol
to pistol." Vest read into the *Congressional Record* a letter
from a Cherokee resident of the Indian Territory, who
described the criminal justice system of the territory as "a
howling farce": "The country is one grand asylum for all the
criminals who choose to accept it as a safe retreat." The letter
writer claimed that Parker had released an accused thief after
the payment of a one-dollar fine, based on a Roman Catholic
priest's testimony that the defendant had done penance and
received absolution. Parker, according to this tale, released
the accused after the payment of a one-dollar fine.

The Major Crimes Act of 1885 diminished the powers of
the tribal courts in the Indian Territory and gave the Fort
Smith, Arkansas; Wichita, Kansas; and Graham, Texas courts
jurisdiction in all cases in which Indians were charged with
the capital crimes of murder and rape. It also took from the
tribal courts jurisdiction over felonies for which Indians could
be sentenced to hard labor: manslaughter, arson, assault with
intent to kill, burglary, and larceny. The tribal courts were
allowed to continue trying cases of lesser offenses in which
both parties were Indians. All else went to the federal district
courts for Western Arkansas, Kansas, and Northern Texas.

In 1889 Congress established a United States District
Court at Muskogee, Indian Territory. Its jurisdiction covered
the territory except for the Chickasaw Nation and the southern part of the Choctaw Nation, over which the court
at Paris, Texas, retained jurisdiction. At the time of the

Muskogee court's creation, whites outnumbered Indians in the territory three to one. Proceedings were to be in English, with translators provided for witnesses who could not speak it. The Muskogee court heard all civil cases involving one hundred dollars or more if at least one of the parties was a United States citizen. In cases in which United States citizens were defendants, the jurors had to be citizens also. The court had criminal jurisdiction, but offenses punishable by death or hard labor where still to be tried at Fort Smith, Paris, or Wichita. So, too, were the cases in which the crimes had been committed before the existence of the Muskogee court.

In 1890 Congress created Oklahoma Territory out of the western part of the Indian Territory. This decision was the product of years of agitation by land-hungry whites and the efforts of the nation's lawmakers to diminish or eliminate the authority of tribal courts and the tribunals at Fort Smith, Paris, and Wichita. Each of the new territory's seven counties was to have a court with both federal and territorial jurisdiction. The same legislation divided the Indian Territory into three judicial divisions and gave them concurrent jurisdiction in liquor cases with the United States courts at Paris and Fort Smith. It also eliminated the jurisdiction of the Kansas federal court, but two years later the new Fort Scott division of the District Court of Kansas was given jurisdiction over major crimes committed in the seven small reservations that made up the Quapaw Agency. In 1895 the Indian Territory divisions became districts, each of which was to have a United States District Court. Finally, the Curtis Act of 1898 abolished the tribal courts and declared that Indian law was unenforceable in federal courts. A small part of Parker's jurisdiction in Arkansas was lost in 1892, when Congress detached Montgomery County and added it to the Eastern District of Arkansas.

The shrinking of the Western District of Arkansas's domain brought little relief for the court at Fort Smith. Its deputy marshals had seldom gone into the land that was now Oklahoma Territory. Also, largely because of the unstoppable influx of whites, crime continued unabated in Parker's

reduced bailiwick. Robert Owen, the United States agent for
the Five Nations, reported in 1887 that the "district court for
the western district of Arkansas has more business than it can
possibly attend to." Owen had not presented several cases to
the court "because of their minor character when compared
to more important criminal matters, and the present embar-
rassment of the court in the multitude of important cases to
hear." The problem was not the judge: "There were few
courts . . . where business is conducted with more celerity or
greater fairness, due largely to the very superior ability and
high character of Hon. Isaac C. Parker."

Statistics show the losing battle. By June 30, 1883, the end
of the fiscal year during which the Fort Smith court lost much
of its jurisdiction, the court had terminated 517 criminal
cases, leaving only 41 pending. A year later, the court had terminated 580 cases, with 63 pending. In the next fiscal year,
the figures rose to 582 and 87, then to 724 and 122. During
this period from 1883 to 1886, the court's expenditures rose
from $160,000 to $250,000. When the court ran out of
money in February 1887, Parker suspended business until
July because Congress had not provided a special appropria-
tion. Meanwhile, he lost the services of many deputies, which
resulted in fewer arrests but no decrease in the caseload. By
1889, after the passage of legislation that left Parker with only
major crimes to handle, he terminated 552 prosecutions and
left 113 pending. Between 1889 and July 1, 1893, Parker's
court decided 3,644 criminal cases and 104 civil cases. The
other federal courts with jurisdiction in the Indian Territory
found themselves similarly overwhelmed.

Expenses continued to be high. For the period from 1889
to 1893, the federal government spent more than a million
dollars to operate the court at Fort Smith. The bill for operations for 1892 to 1893, during which 1,155 criminal cases
were terminated, came to around $288,000.

Even though the reduction of the geographical area of his
judicial control did nothing to lessen Parker's burden, he
fought hard to retain as much of his power as possible. A

number of cases involving jurisdictional disputes between the various courts gave him opportunities to assert claims for his court's continuing authority in the Indian Territory.

A serious and complex example of conflicting jurisdictions was a case involving a band of horse thieves. Deputies from the Paris court pursued the outlaws, who were black, through the Chickasaw and Seminole nations. Following a shoot-out between the lawmen and the thieves in Bruner Town, a freedmen's community on the border of the Creek and Seminole nations, the deputies arrested and jailed several members of the gang. A local man was killed in the fracas. Since the killing occurred within Parker's domain, his court instituted proceedings against the five Texas deputies involved. All five were released following a commissioner's hearing in which the Second Chief of the Seminole Nation appeared in their behalf. The case was reopened at Fort Smith, however. Four deputies were tried in 1893, and all were acquitted.

Another case involving a jurisdictional dispute concerned the persistent land-grabber, David L. Payne. In one of his attempts at white colonization, he and his followers erected a shanty in the area known as the Cherokee Outlet, which had supposedly come under the jurisdiction of the United States District Court of Kansas. Connell Rogers, a clerk of the Union Agency, set fire to the shanty and destroyed it. Rogers was arrested on a charge of arson and taken into custody by the marshal of the Western District of Arkansas. But the Kansas court, believing that the matter was properly within its bailiwick, issued a warrant of removal. At the same time, Rogers petitioned Parker's court for a writ of habeas corpus on the grounds that the Kansas court had no jurisdiction in the Cherokee Outlet.

Parker decided in favor of the petitioner. He ruled that the 1883 law had indeed given the Kansas tribunal jurisdiction over the Outlet, but not those parts of it that had been "*set apart and occupied* [emphasis in the original] by the Cherokee, Creek, and Seminole Indian tribes." He held that it was not necessary for Indians to have actually settled there;

it was, in his view, still "occupied"—that is, owned—by the Cherokee Nation. The Kansas court, therefore, lacked jurisdiction in the lands in question. Parker refused the warrant of removal and discharged Rogers. Here he was not only fighting to retain his authority but also protecting the Indians against the incursions of Payne and his boomers.

Soon afterward, Eighth Circuit Judge David J. Brewer nullified Parker's decision in the Rogers case. In *United States* v. *Soule et al.*, the defendants, who had been accused of murder in the Outlet, argued that the court at Fort Smith, not the Wichita tribunal, had jurisdiction. Brewer ruled to the contrary. He had made a "thorough study" of Parker's "careful and elaborate" opinion in the Rogers matter and had made note of the "distinguished ability of that learned judge." Brewer was, however, "unable to yield to the force of his reasoning." The circuit judge pointed to the "potent geographical fact" that the Outlet was closer to Wichita than to Fort Smith. Surely, he wrote, "convenience and economy of business require that the territory subject to the jurisdiction of a court should be as near as possible to the place where the court is held, and the very distribution of the territory [by the act of 1883] is evidence that congress had this matter of economy and convenience in mind." Moreover, in Brewer's view, the Outlet was intended to be a "passage ground over which the Cherokees might pass to all the unoccupied domains west," not a home to be "occupied." Although Brewer's decision denied Parker's court jurisdiction in the Outlet, it helped confirm Cherokee title to the area.

Although Parker was protective of Indians and their rights, in jurisdictional clashes with the tribal courts, he was determined not to allow encroachments upon his court's prerogatives. An 1878 case, *Ex parte Kenyon*, concerned a white man who had been married to a Cherokee woman. When she died, he moved from the Indian Territory to Kansas, taking a horse with him. When the Cherokee tribal court convicted him of larceny, Kenyon petitioned Parker's court for a writ of habeas corpus. The Cherokee counsel asserted that the district court had "no authority to issue the writ to run in the Indian Territory." Parker emphatically disagreed: "The Cherokee Nation does not certainly possess higher rights of sovereignty than the several states of the Union. If [the states] cannot hold a party in custody or restrain him of his liberty in violation of the Constitution, laws, or treaties of the United States, neither can it be done by the Cherokee Nation." Parker found it inconceivable "that in [the Indian Territory] those persons who might invoke this writ of right if they were out of that country could not receive its benefits because they were in it." Habeas corpus was "the highest right possessed by an American citizen, and in a proper case his right to this writ follows him in the Indian Territory, as well as elsewhere." Because Kenyon had left the Indian Territory and taken up residence in Kansas, the Cherokee court that had convicted him had no jurisdiction and could not imprison him. Accordingly, Parker ordered Kenyon's release.

Historian Sidney L. Harring has called the *Kenyon* decision the "most important jurisdictional ruling" among the many Parker decisions that added up to "a significant extension of U.S. power into the Indian nations." Another historian, Angie Debo, concludes that although the Indians of the Five Nations came to respect Parker "for his firmness and integrity . . . they always hated and feared the jurisdiction of his court." The Indian citizens of the territory believed, with good reason, that the Fort Smith court "paralyzed their action against white intruders" and "hindered their own law enforcement."

Other cases illustrate the point. When a man named Frank Morgan was accused of having murdered the sheriff of Sequoyah County in the Cherokee Nation, he fled to Arkansas. Dennis W. Bushyhead, principal chief of the Cherokees, directed the governor of Arkansas to extradite Morgan. Accordingly, the sheriff of Sebastian County arrested the fugitive. While in the sheriff's custody, Morgan initiated habeas corpus proceedings in the court for the Western District of Arkansas. In his decision granting the writ, Parker held that his court had jurisdiction in the matter because the interpretation of federal laws and the Constitution were involved. He cited the 1846 treaty that said that fugitives from justice from the Cherokee Nation were to be delivered to the Cherokee authorities by the United States, not the states. Since the Cherokee Nation was neither a state nor a territory, the governor of Arkansas had no authority to issue an arrest warrant upon the demand of the principal chief. Finally, Parker pointed out fatal flaws in the affidavit on which the requisition for extradition was based: Bushyhead had not certified it as authentic and it did not show whether Morgan or the murdered man were Indians.

Although Parker had declined to turn Morgan over to Cherokee authorities, he readily handed over to state authorities a horse thief named Elmore. The man had taken property he had stolen in Arkansas into the Indian Territory. There a deputy marshal arrested him and brought him before a United States commissioner at Fort Smith. He admitted guilt and went to jail to await trial, but before Elmore could be indicted, Parker responded to a warrant issued by a justice of the peace in Franklin County, Arkansas, and turned him over to state law enforcement officers. While in the custody of the county sheriff, Elmore entered a plea "alleging that the federal court, having first acquired possession of the case, had exclusive jurisdiction." At his trial he pleaded not guilty, was convicted, and appealed to the supreme court of Arkansas, which ruled, in *Elmore* v. *State* (1885), that the court at Fort Smith had concurrent jurisdiction with the state courts in such cases and that Parker had the authority to surrender Elmore to the state officers. The Arkansas justices maintained that no inquiry was necessary into the legality or illegality "of his capture in a foreign country" because it did not affect jurisdiction. Besides, they found nothing in the record to indicate anything improper about his arrest. The court's opinion concluded with the belief that Elmore was "manifestly guilty, and there is no danger that he will be twice punished for the same offense."

The case *In re Wolf[e]* (1886) further illustrates how Parker imposed federal jurisdiction on Indian tribunals. He saw to it that two Cherokee defendants were tried by a federal court in Washington rather than by a tribal court. The Supreme Court for the District of Columbia indicted Richard M. Wolfe, Robert B. Ross, and William A. Phillips for conspiring to defraud the Cherokee Nation of $22,500 in a sale of lands in the Cherokee Outlet to other tribes. Wolfe and Ross were Cherokee delegates in Washington; Phillips, a former Kansas congressman, was the tribe's special agent and counsel. The two Cherokee delegates were arrested on warrants issued by Commissioner Stephen Wheeler and taken into the custody of the marshal of the Fort Smith court. The court in Washington issued a warrant of removal. Wolfe and Ross petitioned Parker for their release on the grounds that they and the alleged victim, the Cherokee Nation, were Indians, and therefore could only be tried in the Cherokee courts. Parker disagreed: they were accused of having committed the crime in the District of Columbia, and they should be tried there. He required Wolfe and Ross to post a $2,000 bond for their appearance before the court in Washington.

In many of the cases brought before Parker, determining Indian citizenship was a thorny problem. *Ex parte Reynolds*, an 1879 habeas corpus proceeding, illustrates some of the difficulties. Reynolds, a white man, was accused of murdering Puryear, another white man. Both men had married Choctaw women. Reynolds's attorney argued that this made them Indians at law. If so, the court for the Western District of Arkansas lacked jurisdiction because if both parties were citizens of the Choctaw Nation, the case must be tried in a tribal court. Although other courts had held that the condition of the mother defined one's citizenship, Parker chose to follow the rule of international law, as pronounced by the eighteenth-century Swiss authority Emmerich de Vattel: the status of the father determined citizenship. Although the murdered man's wife, Mrs. Puryear, was an Indian, her paternal grandfather was white and a citizen of Mississippi. Therefore,

Parker ruled, her father was a citizen of the United States, as was Mrs. Puryear. Her husband could not then have become a Choctaw by marriage. Since Puryear was a citizen of the United States, the case belonged in the Fort Smith tribunal. Parker accordingly dismissed the writ of habeas corpus. He stated that using the status of the mother to determine citizenship came from the Roman law regarding slavery and should not be applied to free persons. He also noted that statute law and common law were silent as to the degree, or "quantum", of Indian blood for determining whether a person was a citizen of the United States or of an Indian nation.

Another case further reveals Parker's attempt to deal with the question of tribal citizenship and jurisdiction. John Mayfield was convicted in Parker's court of "adultery in the Indian country" and was sentenced to three years in the Detroit House of Correction. He sought a writ of habeas corpus from the United States Supreme Court on the grounds that he was a Cherokee by blood who had lived in the Cherokee Nation all his life and could therefore only be tried by a Cherokee court. The assistant attorney general who argued the case before the Supreme Court asserted that the 1889 act that had created the federal court for the Indian Territory left the Fort Smith court with jurisdiction only over crimes punishable by death or hard labor. The Supreme Court, speaking through Justice Henry Brown, held that legislation of 1890 left cases in which Indians were the only parties within the jurisdiction of the tribal courts: "A member of the Cherokee Nation, committing adultery with an unmarried woman within the limits of its Territory, is amenable only to the courts of the [Cherokee] Nation." The High Court granted the writ and ordered the discharge of the prisoner. *Ex parte Mayfield* (1891) effectively eliminated the question of citizenship as an element affecting jurisdiction in criminal cases arising in the Indian Territory.

In *Ex parte Kyle* (1895), Parker concluded that his court did not have jurisdiction and that a tribal court did. Elijah Kyle, a white man married to an Indian woman, was charged with larceny. He was tried twice in a Cherokee court, and the jury was deadlocked both times. While the case was still pending, the defendant applied to the federal court for the Indian Territory for United States citizenship, as was authorized by a federal statute of 1890. When the Muskogee tribunal granted the application, Kyle applied to Parker for habeas corpus, claiming that as a citizen of the United States he was beyond the reach of the tribal courts. Parker rejected this reasoning and dismissed the writ: "According to my judgment, the petitioner could not divest the Cherokee court of jurisdiction over him in this way." Allowing Kyle to escape the Indian court's jurisdiction by acquiring United States citizenship would permit others to elude punishment by doing the same. Parker went on to praise the criminal justice systems of the Five Nations: "The Indian Nations are making an honest effort to enforce the law, especially for the protection of life. This can be especially said with reference to the Cherokee Nation."

Parker showed the same reluctance to concede jurisdiction to the new federal court for the Indian Territory that he displayed in disputes with the tribal courts and the Kansas federal court. Soon after the creation of the United States Court for Indian Territory in 1889, the new tribunal indicted and convicted James Farley and Robert Wilson of larceny. They sought their freedom by petitioning Parker for habeas corpus. He granted their petitions on the grounds that the law establishing the Indian Territory federal court did not provide for a grand jury; since the court had no authority to impanel a grand jury, the accused could not be indicted by an "illegal body."

In joint proceedings (*Ex parte McClusky*, 1889; and *Ex parte Brown*, 1889), a man and a woman had been convicted of larceny at Muskogee, waived grand jury indictment, and pleaded guilty. They then sought their freedom on habeas corpus in Parker's court. Parker ruled that they were entitled to their liberty because they could not waive their constitutional right to a grand jury hearing. Indictment by a grand jury was required before they could be tried, and the court for the Indian Territory was not authorized to impanel one.

In Parker's view, a citizen's liberty "is a donation of the Great Creator, and cannot be taken by persons upon their own authority, even with the consent of the citizen whose liberty is taken."

In another case, a man convicted of assault in the Indian Territory federal court sought a writ of habeas corpus from Parker. The Fort Smith judge held, in *Ex parte Brown* (1889), not to be confused with the preceding *Brown* case, that the Muskogee tribunal had tried the defendant for assault, a misdemeanor, because it did not have the power to try cases of assault with intent to kill, a felony, which, in Parker's view, was the appropriate charge. "I am satisfied," he said, "that the court at Muskogee had no jurisdiction to try the petitioner of the offense he is really guilty of, and he is therefore entitled to a discharge from arrest." He went on to accuse the Indian Territory court of fashioning the case to give itself jurisdiction. He scolded the federal authorities responsible for this and related injustices: "I desire to say, in regard to all these cases which have been before me on *habeas corpus*, that I think the government has made a mistake. By this mistake, these petitioners have been wrongly deprived of their liberty; they have been harassed by a trial; they have been put to the expense of employing counsel; they have been cast into prison."

In the case of Edward Crawford, the confusion over which federal court had jurisdiction—that for the Indian Territory or that for the Western District of Arkansas—resulted in a miscarriage of justice. He, too, had been convicted of the misdemeanor charge of assault by the court at Muskogee, which imposed only a fine. Parker's court then assumed jurisdiction and, apparently on the same grounds as the foregoing case, tried him on the felony charge of assault with intent to kill and sentenced him to four years in the Detroit House of Correction. Fortunately for Crawford, the matter came to the attention of President Benjamin Harrison. "This man," the president stated, "was tried twice for the same offense and distinct penalties imposed." Harrison acknowledged that perhaps the Indian Territory court should not have heard the case. The president's solution was to commute Crawford's sentence to the five months of prison time already served.

Even when there was cooperation between the Fort Smith bench and the authorities in the Indian nations, justice did not always triumph. Two mixed bloods, Richard Vann and Alfred Cunningham, killed Sam Sixkiller, the respected captain of the Union Agency police and a deputy United States marshal, in the Creek Nation. A Creek court indicted them, but they fled to the Cherokee Nation. Vann was killed, and Cunningham was brought to Fort Smith on a larceny charge. Parker wrote to Dennis W. Bushyhead and Joseph M. Perryman, principal chiefs of the Cherokees and Creeks, and agreed to release Cunningham provided that he be returned to Fort Smith if the Creek court acquitted him of the murder charge.

Because of the seriousness of the crime and the necessity of both chiefs agreeing to Parker's conditions, Parker waived the provision. In a letter to Perryman, he stated that "This case is one of the most important which has been presented in your Courts. The murder was a brutal, barbarous assassination. . . . It has attracted the attention of the whole country. It has been alluded to in debate in the Congress of the United States." Parker duly released Cunningham to the Cherokee authorities, who delivered him to the Creek nation. Cunningham escaped back into the Cherokee country, was caught, and was again extradited. The desperado escaped a second time and was never recaptured.

In many of the habeas corpus proceedings brought before him, Parker appeared to be sensitive to the civil liberties of the petitioners. More evident, however, was his determination, in granting writs of habeas corpus, to cling to what remained of his dwindling jurisdiction. Yet there were instances of his concern for the rights of citizens—as long as the case did not involve protecting his court's authority from intrusions of other jurisdictions. Two connected cases illustrate Parker's desire to safeguard constitutional liberties. A police court in Fort Smith had fined Amanda Marquandt five dollars and costs for a misdemeanor. Because she was unable or unwilling to pay the fine, the police court judge sent her to jail. The mayor ordered her release on the grounds that she was not in good health; she was required to pay only the court costs of one dollar and fifty cents. The police court judge ordered policeman Robert Monroe to rearrest her. He refused and was jailed for contempt. He and Marquandt sought writs of habeas corpus from Parker, who found in their favor. Parker ruled that his court had jurisdiction because the cases involved a federal question: the Fourteenth Amendment rights of the incarcerated pair. He conceded that the police court had the power to punish contempt. A local ordinance, however, allowed the mayor to discharge prisoners for nonpayment of fines if their health was endangered. Monroe, the policeman, was within his rights to refuse to serve the unlawful warrant to recommit Marquandt. Parker further noted that Monroe had been sentenced to twenty-five days in jail, even though Arkansas state law limited punishment for contempt to ten days. The imprisonment of Monroe and Marquandt, therefore, amounted to "restraint of liberty without due process of law," a violation of the Fourteenth Amendment. He ordered the release of both.

Parker also used the Fourteenth Amendment to strike down a Fort Smith ordinance that allowed men walking the streets with disreputable women to be arrested. The judge reasoned that there was no way of knowing with certainty the intentions of two people seen on the streets and that the ordinance was therefore an unconstitutional restraint of liberty.

The Fourteenth Amendment was an issue in a Supreme Court matter that originated in Parker's court. Henry Carter, a black man, was convicted at Fort Smith for having stolen cattle belonging to an Indian. Parker sentenced Carter to prison and, in accordance with the 1834 Intercourse Act, ordered him to pay the owner of the cattle double the value of the stolen property. Carter was unable to pay. The Intercourse Act made the United States treasury liable when the guilty party could not make payment, but the act referred only to instances in which whites were convicted of stealing from Indians. Parker had interpreted "white" to mean "non-Indian." The owner of the stolen property sought payment from the treasury by bringing suit in the United States Court of Claims. A divided court was unable to agree if the changed status of blacks brought about by the Thirteenth and Fourteenth Amendments had made the 1834 act applicable to crimes committed by blacks against Indians. The judges decided pro forma for the claimant so that the case could go to the Supreme Court for a definitive ruling.

The Supreme Court, in *United States* v. *Perryman* (1880), reversed the Court of Claims. The justices decided that there must be strict adherence to the wording of the statute despite the changed status of blacks brought about by the Thirteenth and Fourteenth Amendments. "There may be no good reason for restricting any longer this liability to acts of whites," wrote Chief Justice Morrison R. Waite, "but until Congress sees fit to change the statute in this particular, the courts are not at liberty to disregard the law as it is left to stand."

Presiding over courts outside his district gave Parker the opportunity to hear criminal cases involving tamer offenses than those coming out of the Indian Territory. In the federal court system, the judge of a circuit had the authority to temporarily assign district judges to other districts. Usually this was done when a judge was incapacitated, vacationing, or overburdened, or when a judgeship was temporarily vacant. Parker, despite his crowded docket, was sent at least twice to preside over other tribunals in the Eighth Circuit. In 1892 he was ordered to the Western District of Missouri, where, substituting for Judge John F. Philips, he heard cases in the Springfield and Saint Joseph divisions. Holding court at Saint Joseph brought him back to the community where he had begun his legal career.

Unlike Fort Smith, the docket of the Western District of Missouri consisted mostly of civil cases, and the few criminal cases seldom involved violence. One of the criminal actions brought before Parker in Saint Joseph concerned a violation of the Interstate Commerce Act of 1887, which was, Parker stated, a law that embodied "great wisdom" because it attempted to protect the public from the machinations of large shippers. Three defendants were accused of conspiring to obtain favorable shipping rates for lumber, one of them being a railroad employee who allegedly underweighed the lumber. During the trial the district attorney dropped charges against one defendant, but the jury found the remaining two guilty. Parker sentenced them to one and a half years in prison. They appealed to the Supreme Court (*Howell et al.* v. *United States*, 1896). On the authority of counsel for the plaintiffs in error, the solicitor general entered a motion to dismiss the case, which the Court did, leaving the verdict of Parker's court intact.

Like those who faced the hangman's noose, many people convicted of noncapital offenses also applied for executive clemency. Parker occasionally recommended clemency, yet he did not make a habit of interceding on behalf of those found guilty in his court. When Grover Cleveland pardoned counterfeiter Mike Warren, he rejected the prisoner's pleas of innocence and ill-health, basing his action instead on Parker's belief that the prisoner had suffered enough. "This judge," said Cleveland, "is so little given to recommending pardons that in this case I think I am safe in following his judgment." As in cases of persons convicted of capital crimes, it is likely that Parker often urged the rejection of petitions for clemency by those convicted of noncapital crimes.

After murder and rape, the most serious crimes of violence were manslaughter and assault with intent to kill. Parker, usually along with the district attorney and others, sought clemency for several men imprisoned on these charges. Most commonly, he cited "provocation" (and sometimes "great" or "extreme" provocation) as the reason for urging a pardon or commutation. Sometimes he believed that there were "mitigating circumstances" or that the "killing was excusable." In the case of William Frazier, it was "because of the desperate wounds received at time of arrest, which unfit him for imprisonment." Samuel Still was only "technically guilty"

of assault with intent to kill and had "suffered enough."
Joseph Jackson, convicted of manslaughter, received a pardon
upon the recommendations of Parker and the district attorney. They had doubts as to intentional homicide because
Jackson had apparently been "attempting to defend his
mother from the violent assaults of her brutal and drunken
husband." Pinkey Hanks, convicted of assault with intent to
kill, received a pardon because the judge and district attorney
believed there had been "much provocation."

In still another case, Thomas Knight, who was a lieutenant
of the Union Agency's police, and two Texas Rangers killed a
desperado in the Choctaw Nation who had violently resisted
arrest. The three men were found guilty of manslaughter in a
trial before Parker. Clearly, they had killed in self-defense, but
the jury was apparently influenced by the fact that they had
no authority to arrest the man they had killed. Parker, with
dubious legality, suspended their sentences, and Grover
Cleveland pardoned them.

Others who obtained pardons or reduced sentences based
in part on Parker's intercession included people sent to prison
for bribery, impersonating a federal officer, larceny, and violations of the liquor, postal, and pension laws. John S. Percy,
convicted of receiving stolen goods, was pardoned because
Parker and the district attorney said there was "a doubt if he
knew the goods were stolen." The judge and the prosecutor
also believed that Samuel Waters, convicted for accepting a
bribe from a prisoner in his charge, should be freed because
of the bad character of the witnesses against him and "grave
doubts of his guilt." Convicted thief Samuel Watkins secured
his freedom because Parker and the district attorney pointed
out that the convict's wife had died, leaving four small children to be cared for; here, too, there was "grave doubt as to
his guilt." Parker and the prosecuting attorney were of the
opinion that Albert Gamble, behind bars for introducing
alcohol into the Indian country, was entitled to be freed
because at his trial "the facts were exaggerated." Many people were pardoned, with or without Parker's intercession,

because of impaired physical or mental health, previous good character, good conduct in prison, or the need to have their rights of citizenship restored.

As President Cleveland observed, Parker recommended fewer pardons than most federal judges. Nevertheless, the instances in which Parker supported commutation or pardon show that he was capable of compassion. Stern though he was in his remarks on and off the bench, Parker believed that no one was beyond redemption. When he saw the faces of the many men he had sentenced, he felt that none "had entirely lost that better part of human nature which makes a man a good citizen, and a faint spark of which lingers in the nature of the worst and most depraved convict." "The object of punishment," he believed, was "to lift the man up, to stamp out his bad nature and wicked disposition, that his better and God given traits may assert themselves."

When David J. Brewer, judge of the Eighth Circuit, was elevated to the Supreme Court in 1889, there was a movement to urge President Harrison to appoint Parker to fill the vacancy. The judge permitted his well-wishers to write to the president on his behalf. Attorney General William H. H. Miller assured Parker that he was glad to submit his name for consideration. Soon, however, voices were raised in opposition. Parker responded with letters to Miller and Harrison denouncing those who were working to block his nomination, labeling one of his more vociferous critics a "naturalized Judas." Nevertheless, he asked that his name be withdrawn from consideration, and Henry C. Caldwell was named to succeed Brewer as circuit judge. This left a vacancy on the United States District Court for the Eastern District of Arkansas. President Harrison offered Parker the post. Overworked though Parker was, he declined the less demanding position, stating that his present judicial post was among the most important in the nation.

The whittling away of his jurisdiction had not brought any relief in Parker's heavy judicial responsibilities, yet some developments made his situation less onerous. After years of complaints from the marshals, grand juries, attorneys general, the press, and Parker himself, Congress appropriated fifty thousand dollars to build a new jail at Fort Smith, which was completed in 1887. This action was a response to a national movement for prison reform as well as a result of the old jail's notoriety throughout the country. Attorney General Augustus H. Garland, in 1885, had called it "the most miserable prison, probably, in the whole country." A three-story brick structure with seventy-two cells now replaced the odious dungeon beneath the courtroom. On March 19, 1888, the marshal moved the prisoners to the new federal jail. Inmates guilty of capital crimes occupied the ground level; women and those convicted of larceny and assault occupied the second floor; liquor offenders occupied the third floor.

Although the new jail was an improvement, it was soon apparent that it was too small. In 1895 Marshal George Crump informed Attorney General Judson Harmon that the jail's population averaged between 185 and 220 prisoners, most of them representative of "the worst class of criminals." Among them were, he estimated, 20 convicted murderers, 15 awaiting trial for murder, and the remainder "train robbers, horse thieves and such like characters." Moreover, the jail's faulty construction encouraged escape attempts such as that of Crawford Goldsby.

Of more direct benefit to Parker was the removal of his court from the former barracks to the third floor of Fort Smith's new federal building three blocks away. Parker opened the February 1890 session of the court in this more suitable facility. The former barracks continued to house the offices of the United States commissioner, marshal, and jailer, and part of the old building was used as a hospital for the prisoners.

Also making life more bearable was an increase in Parker's salary. In the early 1890s his annual income rose from $3,500 to $5,000. Another factor that probably influenced Parker's decision to remain in Fort Smith was that he and his family had long been respected and comfortable in the community and much involved in its affairs.

The new jail for the Western District of Arkansas, built in 1889. The old courthouse is on the right. *Fort Smith National Historic Site.*

CHAPTER 5

Between Man and Man

ON more than one occasion, Isaac Parker expressed contempt for civil law. Cases that arose out of "controversies
between man and man," he told a grand jury, had come to be
"regarded of much more importance than the enforcement of
the law which protects the life of the citizen." Criminal law
had "fallen rather into disgrace," especially in the larger cities.
"Now," he asked, "is it not more important to protect a
man's life than it is his property?" A man could lose all of his
money or property, Parker said, and still be able to survive
and perhaps recoup his losses, but loss of life was irremedia-
ble. At another time he blamed the hegemony of civil law on
the materialism of the times: "Avarice, which is the curse of
the age, has so poisoned the people that civil law for the protection of property concerns it more than the criminal law
which protects life."

For all of Parker's supposed disdain for the branch of law
that concerned disputes between citizens, he had no choice
but to hear the civil cases that came before his court. And to
ignore them, as most historians have, is to miss an important
part of his total record as a jurist and his responses to some of
the major legal issues of the day.

Compared with other federal courts, Parker's civil caseload
was unusually light. One reason for the relatively few civil
actions is that potential litigants in the far reaches of the
Indian Territory had to travel great distances to bring suit in
Fort Smith. This was especially true before 1883, when the
court's jurisdiction encompassed all of the Indian Territory.
Rather than make the long and expensive trip to Arkansas, the

disputing parties often settled the issue themselves—sometimes violently—or submitted the matter to an Indian agent
for arbitration.

Congressional legislation of 1891 had an impact on
Parker's civil jurisdiction. That year, to relieve the Supreme
Court of some of its burden, Congress created the Circuit
Courts of Appeals, one for each of the nine federal circuits.
Cases decided in district and circuit courts could be taken to
the new appellate courts. These intermediate tribunals had
final jurisdiction over diversity cases, that is, those in which
the opposing parties were citizens of different states. The new
courts of appeals freed the Supreme Court to hear only cases
that called for interpretation of federal statutes, treaties, and
the Constitution. The 1891 law also provided for the appointment of a second circuit judge to each of the nine federal circuits; these two judges plus a district judge would sit as the
judges of the new appellate courts. The act kept the old circuit courts but took away their appellate jurisdiction.

Civil cases under appeal from the Western District of
Arkansas now went to the Court of Appeals for the Eighth
Circuit in Saint Louis. All of the cases taken there from
Parker's court were civil actions because the new tribunals'
criminal jurisdiction was limited to appeals from convictions
for lesser crimes, and since 1889, the federal court at Muskogee had been handling these cases in the Indian Territory.
Appeals of death or hard labor sentences went directly from
the lower courts to the Supreme Court. So did civil cases
involving jurisdictional questions.

At first, the civil suits on Parker's docket came almost
entirely from the counties of western Arkansas. The few civil
cases coming out of the Indian Territory were limited to constitutional questions, such as the property rights of people
whose liquor had been confiscated by the deputy marshals or,
as noted earlier, the destruction of a shanty erected by David
L. Payne and his boomers. A significant change came in
1884, when Congress allowed Indian tribes and individual
residents of the Indian Territory to sue or be sued by the rail-

roads that had been granted rights of way in the territory. For such cases, the federal courts in Paris, Fort Scott, and Fort Smith were given concurrent jurisdiction.

The Cherokees objected to the granting of railroad franchises other than the two that had been specifically authorized by treaties. They brought suit (*Cherokee Nation* v. *Southern Kansas Railway Co.*, 1890) in Parker's court, seeking damages and an injunction to block the taking of tribal land for the railroads. The tribe's attorneys argued that the federal government's power of eminent domain did not extend to the tribal lands. Parker ruled that the Indian nations were not exempt from the federal exercise of eminent domain because the federal government, not the nations, was sovereign in the Indian Territory. Parker further stated that the Cherokee Nation should not have joined their suit for recovery of damages, a proceeding in law, with their petition for an injunction, a proceeding in equity.

Tribal officials appealed to the Supreme Court, which reversed Parker's decision. Speaking through Justice John Marshall Harlan, the Court's opinion stated that although Parker was correct in ruling that two causes (one equitable, the other legal) could not be united in the same suit, "the court below ought not . . . to have dismissed the plaintiff out of court, without making some provision, by appropriate orders, for the protection of its rights as against the railroad company." According to Harlan, Parker should have treated the complaint "as a petition of appeal which entitled the [Cherokees] to have a trial *de novo* on the questions of damages for the lands and rights proposed to be taken." Nevertheless, the justices upheld Parker on an important point, the federal government's power of eminent domain in the Indian Territory.

Congress and the state legislatures that chartered railroads did not directly exercise the power of eminent domain; rather, they delegated to the railroads the authority to condemn such property as they needed for their rights of way. The owners of the condemned property were supposed to receive fair compensation. In one situation, the St. Louis and San Francisco, or Frisco, railroad took and paid for property in Fort Smith belonging to Mary A. Foltz. She disputed the company's authority to do so. In an 1892 decision, Parker ruled against her, even though the railroad company had not yet used the land in question. He held that there was no doubt that the company had the power of eminent domain. The Foltz case went to the Circuit Court of Appeals in 1894. This court, in an opinion by Judge Walter H. Sanborn, upheld Parker, stating that the Fort Smith court had jurisdiction in such cases and that Parker was correct in deciding for the railroad.

On the other hand, Parker recognized limits to the railroads' exercise of eminent domain. When the Kansas and Arkansas Valley Railway erected a bridge across the Arkansas River linking Fort Smith and the Indian Territory, the railroad company attempted to condemn land on the territory side to build a road for foot and passenger traffic leading to the bridge. Two Cherokees operating a ferry company, Gabriel and Houston Payne, sought an injunction to prevent the condemning of their property for the road. The Paynes claimed that the roadway "would utterly destroy the value of the ferry privilege [granted to them by the Cherokee Nation] . . . and cause almost a total loss . . . of the money invested in said ferry, ferry franchises, privileges, and other ferry property." After issuing a temporary restraining order against the railroad, Parker handed down a decision favoring the Cherokee ferry owners. Congress, he said, had granted the railroad corporation the power of eminent domain, but only for the acquiring of land to build its rail, telephone, and telegraph lines. The power did not extend to condemning private property for the building of a foot and wagon approach to the bridge. He regretted that Congress had neglected to give the railroad the authority to condemn lands for the construction of the roadway, because it caused a "delay in the completion of a great thoroughfare, which will be an important agency in securing the development, progress, and prosperity of the country, and consequently of great and lasting benefit to the people." Although the interests of the Cherokee plaintiffs were small in comparison with those of the corporation, "they must receive the full measure of protection afforded by the law."

Unfortunately for the Paynes, the railroad secured a reversal in the Circuit Court of Appeals. Judge Amos M. Thayer's opinion held that Parker's injunction was too broad because it denied the railroad the only possible access to the bridge. The court agreed that Congress had not expressly granted the power to condemn lands for a roadway, but ruled that the power was implied. Thayer added that Congress intended that the railroad's right of way "should be used by wagons and foot-passengers to such an extent as might be found necessary to enable them to reach the bridge." Any other conclusion would mean that Congress had "granted a right that cannot be enjoyed." The appellate court then annulled and vacated the injunction and remanded the case to the lower court with instructions to take a bond, not to exceed $2,500, to compensate the Paynes for "damages, if any, that might be awarded by a court." On the same grounds, the court also reversed Parker's decision in a companion case, *Kansas and Arkansas Valley Railway Co. v. Le Flore.*

The St. Louis and San Francisco corporation was a party to an even more controversial case. The tribal governments of the Indian Nations entered into an agreement with the railroad that allowed the tribal courts to arbitrate damage claims against the Frisco. The right to enter into such an agreement was challenged in a case brought before Parker. He ruled that the treaties between the tribes and the government that allowed the railroad to build through the Indian lands "did not foresee any agreement to submit claims to Indian courts." But Parker admitted that it was a "proposition startling in its character, that the citizens of the Indian country had no remedy in their courts against this railroad company." Courts, he concluded, "cannot make the law. They must take it as they find it."

Other Parker decisions likewise disappointed citizens of the Indian nations. Throughout the last one-third of the nineteenth century, cattlemen from Texas and Arkansas drove their herds through the Indian Territory to the railheads in Kansas. Federal law imposed a penalty of one dollar per head for stock driven through tribal lands without consent. In 1881 the Creek and Cherokee nations enacted measures that made their consent contingent upon the payment of a tax of ten cents a head on all horses and cattle passing through their lands. When the constitutionality of the taxes were challenged in Parker's court, he held that they were infringements upon Congress's power to regulate interstate commerce. A Creek statute of 1882 authorized the seizure of stock illegally occupying the tribe's lands and allowed the owners of the stock to reclaim their property upon payment of a fine. Parker struck down this measure, too. In an earlier decision, in 1876, he denied Indian officials the right to confiscate the property of whites illegally residing in the territory. "The mere fact of a man being in the Indian country without a permit is no excuse for seizing his property." These decisions, Angie Debo writes, left the Indians "with only the non-existent protection of the Intercourse Acts."

An 1891 civil action, *United States ex rel. McIntosh et al.* v. *Crawford et al.*, was in many respects similar to the earlier habeas corpus case *In re Wolf [e]* (1886). Both involved accusations of wrongdoing by Indians and their white attorneys in the cession of tribal lands. The results in the later case, however, were quite different. In February 1885, delegates of the Creek Nation entered into a contract with attorney Samuel J. Crawford, former governor of Kansas, entrusting him to negotiate with the federal government for the sale of the tribe's western or "Oklahoma" lands. Crawford was to receive as a commission ten percent of the sale price. In March, Congress authorized the purchase by the federal government of the western lands of the Creeks and Seminoles, but a resolution issued by the Five Nations protested against any change in the status of the lands in question. Meanwhile,

word of the Crawford contract leaked out, and the principal
chief of the Creeks informed the secretary of the interior that
the tribe did not consider the contract valid. The secretary
thereupon disapproved it.

A few years later, a new set of Creek delegates, Pleasant
Porter, David M. Hodge, and Isparhecher, revived the
Crawford contract. With the approval of the Creek national
council, Crawford negotiated the sale of the Creek western
lands for $2,280,887.10. The articles of cession provided that
the money be kept in a Creek account in the United States
Treasury, where it would draw five percent per annum, and
that the agent negotiating the agreement be granted ten percent of the sale price. News that Crawford was to get such a
large commission angered tribal members and caused dissen-
sion among their leaders. It was widely believed that the commission ostensibly intended for Crawford was going to be
divided among Porter, Hodge, Isparhecher, and others.
Porter had handled the money and acknowledged that he had
not yet paid Crawford, but, said Porter, "as per verbal agreement, he [Crawford] directed and authorized me to pay it to
others, which I did." He denied that he or the other delegates
had received any of the funds, but declined to say who the
"others" were.

This shady-appearing business came before Parker in a case
brought by the United States on the relation of Daniel N.
McIntosh and other Creek leaders. It was a suit in which the
United States government was seeking to recover the money
the delegates kept. Attorneys for the United States accused
Crawford, his associate Clarence W. Turner, and the three
delegates, with "wicked and unlawful intent, to cheat and
defraud the Creek Nation." Perhaps reluctantly, Parker dismissed the case. First, he ruled that the marshal of the District
of Columbia had no power to serve a writ of summons on
Crawford, a citizen of Kansas, compelling him to appear in
the court for the Western District of Arkansas. On a more
important question, he found that his court lacked jurisdiction to hear the case because Congress had passed a law in

1889 that, Parker said, repealed by implication earlier legislation requiring the consent of the secretary of the interior and
the commissioner of Indian affairs for contracts between
Indian tribes and attorneys and agents acting on their behalf.
The case brought by the government, Parker concluded,
therefore lacked the subject matter needed for the court to
proceed further.

A good deal of the civil litigation brought to Parker's court
involved accidental deaths and injuries. Parker heard many
cases involving persons injured or killed by trains. It was an
enormous national problem. By the 1890s, railroads accounted for six thousand to seven thousand deaths and thirty thousand to forty thousand injuries each year. About one-third of
those killed and two-thirds of those suffering injuries were
railroad employees.

At first, recovering damages was difficult. Railroad attorneys were often successful in persuading judges and juries
that the injured party had by his own negligence contributed
to the accident and was therefore not entitled to compensation. For railroad and other workers, another formidable bar-
rier to collecting damages was the "fellow-servant" rule laid
down by courts earlier in the century. This doctrine held that
if another employee's actions had caused the injury, the
injured party's only recourse was to sue his fellow servant, not
the company. Another doctrine that made it hard to get restitution was "assumption of risk": a person taking employment
in a dangerous workplace did so with the knowledge that
such work jeopardized life and limb.

Public reaction to these doctrines, which obviously favored
railroads and other employers, led to demands that state legislatures modify them. Many states did so in the late nineteenth and early twentieth centuries. Courts themselves also
did much to change the law by laying down new doctrines
that gave the injured parties a better chance for restitution.
The "vice-principal" rule, championed by Stephen J. Field of
the United States Supreme Court, was gaining acceptance
throughout the late nineteenth century. This rule held that if

it could be proved that the fellow employee contributing to the injury was a person of any authority, such as a foreman or even a "straw boss," he was a vice-principal of the employer, thus making the employer liable for damages. Also giving the plaintiffs an edge was the tendency of juries to find in their favor. Many jurors were biased against railroads and other corporations, and thought that even if the company was not entirely responsible for an injury, it could well afford to pay compensation.

It was essential for judges like Parker in this period to instruct juries carefully in the niceties of the legal doctrines governing the awarding of damages. Questions of jurisdiction were also frequently involved. Federal courts heard many personal injury suits brought against railroads because it often happened that the party seeking damages was a citizen of one state and the defendant railroad a corporate citizen of another. Cases that entailed "diversity of citizenship" belonged in the federal circuit courts. In his capacity as circuit judge, Parker heard a good many railroad injury cases.

In one suit, Gerhard Schumacher, a laborer on the St. Louis and San Francisco's line in the Indian Territory, lost a leg as a result of an accident. He sued for fifteen thousand dollars, and the jury awarded him eight thousand dollars. The railroad returned to court (*S[c]humacher* v. *St. Louis and San Francisco Railway Co.*, 1889) and asked for a new trial, claiming that Parker's instructions to the jury had been erroneous. The judge responded that there was nothing wrong with his instructions. He acknowledged that the plaintiff had been "imprudent" when he chose to sit on an open gravel car rather than the caboose, which he had been told was safer. Nevertheless, Parker was firm in his belief that the conductor of the train had been grossly negligent, so much so that his actions were "equivalent to intentional mischief." The conductor had caused the release of ten cars from the engine, sending them hurtling down a grade to collide with the gravel car. This incident, said Parker, "indicated such a degree of indifference to the rights of others . . . as to leave no place for the doctrine of 'contributory negligence'. . . . The fact that one has carelessly put himself in a place of danger is never an excuse for another purposely or recklessly injuring him."

The railroad attorneys also claimed that the award of eight thousand dollars was excessive. Parker responded that he was "at one time inclined to the opinion that the damages were excessive," but he believed that "a court cannot interfere with a verdict on the ground of excessive damages, unless such damages are so excessively large and disproportionate as to warrant the inference that the jury was swayed by prejudice, preference, partiality, passion or corruption." In a later case he insisted that this rule was correct and that it was based on his "full investigation of the older authorities." In the conclusion of the S[c]humacher opinion he expressed his belief that to secure "just results," federal courts were obliged to "put aside all the mere technicalities of the law. They are brushed out of the way as so many cobwebs." Unfortunately for the injured man, the Supreme Court overturned the verdict. Justice Henry B. Brown's opinion held that Schumacher's contributory negligence outweighed any negligence on the railroad's part and that the judge should have directed the jury to find for the railroad. Parker expressed his regret that the case had been reversed by the Supreme Court "right in the face of the law and the facts."

In another case, the family of James Dwyer, a Frisco employee killed on the job, won a substantial award from the jury. In a motion for a new trial, the railroad argued that the $17,820 in damages was excessive and that Parker had erred in several instances. The Fort Smith jurist forcefully and eloquently disagreed. Excessive damages, he stated, were awards based on "passion or prejudice" and were "shocking to the sense of justice" or "unreasonably large." He asked, "Is that the case here?" He pointed out that the deceased was an experienced yardmaster who had been "prudent, sober, industrious, careful with his earnings, devoted to his occupation, faithful in all respects to his family." Dwyer, a strong, healthy man, had been earning $85 to $90 per month.

Evidence indicated that he could reasonably have been expected to live another thirty-two years. At $85 per month, this would amount to $32,640. Subtracting ten years "for old age, disability, and loss of time" reduced the years of future earnings to twenty-two and the amount to $22,440. "Making a liberal allowance for present payment, that is, for discounting the price of a human life, and when you take what the jury found, you do not have an amount shocking to the sense of justice." Parker concluded by denying the railroad's motion for a new trial.

Parker lamented that damage awards in such cases were limited by a "barbaric, and almost brutal" statute that prohibited the jury from taking into consideration "that terrible agony, grief, and suffering of the faithful wife and little children for their loss by death of such a husband and father." The award, therefore, should be "fairly compensatory" and "made with a reasonably liberal spirit." He continued with another attack on the law governing the awards: "Under this statute, a man is considered only as an animal, a beast of burden, like a horse or a mule, with nothing to be considered when he is killed by negligence but his earning capacity."

Among the civil cases tried in Parker's circuit court were *Bennett v. St. Louis & San Francisco Railway Co.* (1895) and four companion cases, brought against the Frisco by the families of employees of the railroad and of a lumber company. All had been killed in the same accident, and the plaintiffs alleged that the Frisco's negligence had caused the deaths. In each case, the jury awarded damages. The railroad's attorneys filed a motion for a new trial, arguing that the "amount of the recovery was excessive, appearing to have been given under the influence of prejudice and passion."

In rejecting the motion, Parker voiced his disapproval of "a very great tendency" of courts to overturn jury verdicts because the judges believed the damages awarded were excessive. He opposed this trend because, he explained, he had confidence in the jury system. Often a judge was "not half as competent to say what amount of damages is proper as is a sensible, plain, ordinary jury composed of the people of the country." As for the case at hand, Bennett had been "literally crushed to pieces, his legs mashed into a jelly" and had lingered for nearly twenty hours in terrible pain before dying. "And for me to sit here and measure the amount of suffering . . . that that man endured in that time in such a way as to say that the jury when they found for that suffering the sum of $6,000.00 that they were swayed by prejudice, preference, partiality, passion or corrupting [*sic*], is a thing I do not think I would be authorized to do."

The Circuit Court of Appeals, in opinions written by Walter H. Sanborn, reversed all five cases. The appellate judges chastised Parker for allowing counsel for the plaintiffs to "indulge in extended discussions of questions not presented by the evidence." The attorneys' histrionics tended to "mislead the jury and to prevent a fair and impartial trial of the case." For this reason, and for the trial judge's erroneous instructions to the jury, the cases were remanded to the lower court for retrial.

The new trials in the Circuit Court for the Western District of Arkansas again resulted in verdicts for the plaintiffs and new appeals to the court at Saint Louis. This time the judges found no fault in Parker's instructions and upheld the jury's awards of damages. The appellate court found that the men who had been killed were not trespassing on the railroad's property and that the railroad had been grossly negligent. The only criticism of Parker's conduct in the second trial was that he had "permitted a material fact to be proven in greater detail than was perhaps necessary."

An Indian Territory employee of the Choctaw Coal and Railway Company was likewise successful in securing a favorable result from a Fort Smith jury. Gowen, one of the receivers of the railroad company, took the case (*Gowen* v. *Harley*) to the Circuit Court of Appeals and obtained a reversal. In an opinion delivered by Judge Sanborn, he and his colleagues held that Parker should have instructed the jury to find for Gowen, the defendant, because, in their view, the injury was the result of the negligence of the plaintiff and a fellow servant. "We think the jury should have been instructed that there was no evidence in this case of any breach of duty on the part of the defendant, and that for this reason they must return a verdict in his favor."

In their decision in the *Gowen* case, the appellate judges agreed with Parker on one point. A congressional statute of 1888 had given the federal courts of Western Arkansas and Northern Texas concurrent jurisdiction in suits between the Choctaw Coal and Railway Company and the Indian tribes. Counsel for the company argued that the act of 1889 creating a circuit court for the Western District of Arkansas had repealed the 1888 statute. The appellate court ruled that it had not.

In *Western Coal & Mining Co.* v. *Ingraham*, the Circuit Court of Appeals affirmed the verdict of the jury that found for an injured worker. Judge Henry C. Caldwell, former judge for the Eastern and Western Districts of Arkansas and now a member of this court, wrote an opinion holding that the fellow-servant rule did not apply in this case and that Parker's instructions to the jury were correct on this point.

Caldwell also agreed with Parker in *St. Louis & San Francisco Railway* v. *Whittle et al.* Bettie Whittle and her sons, Charlie and Frank, sued in the lower court, charging that the death of her husband, W. L. Whittle, who was killed while trying to board a train in the Indian Territory in the dark, was the result of the railroad's negligence. In his jury charge, Parker stated that negligence by the deceased did not prevent an award of damages if the company was also negligent. The verdict was for the Whittles, and the railroad appealed.

Judge Thayer, speaking for himself and Judge Sanborn, reversed the Fort Smith court, holding that Parker's instructions were erroneous and that the verdict was wrong: "We think that the undisputed evidence contained in the present record shows that the deceased was guilty of an act of negligence, which directly contributed to his death." In a spirited dissent, Caldwell wrote that there was no error in the instructions of "the learned and experienced trial judge." He wondered how his colleagues could have reached their decision after fourteen men (the jurors, Parker, and himself) had found no convincing evidence of contributory negligence by Whittle.

Caldwell chastised his brethren for "an invasion of the province of the jury" because they based their decision on their own interpretation of the facts. He expressed his opposition to a recent tendency for courts "to impinge on the functions of the jury and the constitutional rights of suitors." Caldwell disagreed with the "unfounded assumption" used to justify the trend, which was that juries were prejudiced against the corporations that were becoming increasingly powerful in American life. Juries were unable to defend themselves against this charge, wrote Caldwell, but if they could, "they would probably content themselves with a reference to the 'mote' and the 'beam,' with an earnest asseveration that the beam was not in their eye." Caldwell credited jury verdicts with a decrease in the number of damage suits because they forced corporations to exercise greater care and responsibility in their operations.

The railroads (most often the Frisco) taken to Parker's court in personal injury suits regularly raised the jurisdictional question, usually without success. As in so many of the criminal cases in which jurisdiction was challenged, Parker was quick to reply that his was the proper tribunal to hear the case. In *Stephens* v. *St. Louis & San Francisco Railway Co.* (1891), the plaintiff, an Arkansas man, alleged that employees of the Frisco had "struck, beat, kicked, choked, and wounded him . . . tore his clothes, and prevented him from riding in defendant's cars." The railroad contended that the case did not belong in a federal circuit court. Counsel for the railroad cited an Arkansas statute of 1889 that required foreign (that is, out of state) corporations doing business in Arkansas to be incorporated there also, and since the plaintiff and the defendant were both citizens of Arkansas, there was no true diversity of citizenship. Parker rejected this reasoning and ruled that the Frisco, although it had been "adopted as a corporation of Arkansas," was still incorporated in Missouri.

The Arkansas incorporation law was at issue in another 1891 case. This time the matter was not so easily resolved and Parker appears inconsistent. Matthew James, a fireman on the Frisco, was killed in Missouri, on a line that ran from Monett, Missouri, to Fort Smith. His widow, Etta, a citizen of Missouri, claimed that her husband's death was the result of the railroad's negligence. Apparently "shopping" for an amenable judge, jury, or both, Etta James's attorneys took the case to the circuit court at Fort Smith. They claimed diversity of citizenship on the grounds that the railroad was an Arkansas corporation. Counsel for the railroad argued that both the plaintiff and the defendant were citizens of Missouri and that the case could only be decided there. This time Parker accepted the argument that the railroad was a "resident of this judicial district" and heard the case.

The jury awarded Etta James five thousand dollars, and the railroad appealed. The federal act of 1889 entitled the losing party in a circuit court case to take the matter to the Supreme Court if there was a question of jurisdiction. The judges of the Circuit Court of Appeals accordingly sent *St. Louis & San Francisco Railway Co. v. James* to the justices in Washington. The High Court, speaking through Justice George Shiras, reversed Parker, holding that the railroad was a citizen of Missouri alone and that the case, lacking diversity of citizenship, should not have come to the court at Fort Smith. Justice Harlan, in a long dissenting opinion, expressed his agreement with Parker that the corporation was a citizen of Arkansas also.

The Arkansas statute that compelled foreign corporations to be incorporated in the state was enacted precisely to allow citizens of Arkansas to sue railroads in the state courts rather than have such cases go to federal courts on diversity grounds. The justification behind the law was the belief that federal courts tended to be more favorable to railroads and other corporate interests than state courts. Ironically, counsel for Etta James used the law to put the case before Parker's federal court, in the apparent expectation that they would get a more sympathetic hearing there than in the state courts of Missouri.

Another case brought before the Supreme Court on a jurisdictional question was *Briscoe* v. *Southern Kansas Railway Co.* Briscoe, an inhabitant of the Chickasaw Nation, sought damages for the killing of his horses, claiming that the railroad's carelessness was responsible for his loss. He recovered a judgment of $896.75 in Parker's circuit court. The railroad asked for a new trial. At issue was the 1884 act of Congress that authorized the Southern Kansas to build lines in the Indian Territory. The statute gave the federal courts for northern Texas, Kansas, and western Arkansas concurrent jurisdiction over controversies arising between the railroad company and the Indian tribes and nations whose lands were affected. The Southern Kansas corporation argued that the act limited the cases that could be heard in the federal courts to those relating to right of way. It also objected to Parker's refusal to instruct the jury that Briscoe was not an inhabitant of the Chickasaw Nation. Finally, the railroad maintained that it was not responsible for the alleged negligence because its lessee, the Atchison, Topeka and Santa Fe, operated the Southern Kansas's lines in the Indian Territory.

Parker rejected all of these arguments and denied the motion for a new trial. He held that the case belonged in a federal court because the interpretation of the act of 1884 was a federal question. He further ruled that there was sufficient evidence to show that the plaintiff inhabited the Chickasaw Nation. As for the company's attempts to absolve itself by foisting responsibility onto the Santa Fe, the judge said that the lease to the Santa Fe was not authorized by law and was therefore null and void. He punched holes in the Southern Kansas railroad's contention that it could be sued only in cases involving right of way. Did Congress, he asked, intend that the corporation have a franchise that "gave it the right to build its road, own it, run it, and receive its earnings, and the lawful residents of this country . . . were to be left without a remedy for an injury to personal property . . . caused by the negligent and tortious conduct of the defendant's agents? This is hardly to be presumed." The Southern Kansas appealed to the Supreme Court. Chief Justice Melville W. Fuller's opinion for a unanimous Court upheld Parker in every particular.

Another case that fared well on appeal to the nation's highest court was *St. Louis & San Francisco Railway Co.* v. *McBride et al.* Lucy McBride and her children, citizens of Arkansas, alleged that the railroad's negligence had caused the death of her husband, an employee of the company, in an accident that occurred in the Indian Territory. The jury in Parker's circuit court awarded four thousand dollars in damages. The Frisco brought the matter before the Supreme Court, arguing that the Fort Smith tribunal had lacked jurisdiction to hear the case. The railroad's attorneys based their argument on provisions of the 1890 statute regarding the courts of the Indian and Oklahoma Territories that, they contended, made such a case actionable in the state courts of Missouri, the corporate home of the company. Another objection was that the service of process, to a railway station agent in Fort Smith, was defective. The Court, in an opinion delivered by Justice David J. Brewer, rejected these assertions. First, it was clearly a diversity case and therefore properly taken to the Fort Smith circuit court. Brewer stated that, by appearing in the circuit court and arguing the case on its merits, the company had waived any objections on jurisdictional grounds and to defective service of process.

For many years historians have assumed that the American judiciary of the late nineteenth century—federal judges in particular—favored and protected railroads and other corporations. Recent scholarship has modified the assumption and has demonstrated that the federal courts, including the Supreme Court, upheld the great majority of state and federal laws designed to regulate railroad rates and practices. There does not appear to be any major case in Parker's court challenging regulatory laws and their implementation. In railroad injury cases, however, the record indicates he was no friend of the corporations.

Parker directly addressed the notion of the supposed pro-corporate bias of federal courts in a case heard in 1889, *Hoover* v. *Crawford County*. At issue was an Arkansas law of 1879 that was evidently passed to prevent federal courts from hearing suits against the counties of the state. "This act," Parker stated, "seems to me to be but an exhibition of a foolish and futile purpose founded on an unwarrantable and unreasonable prejudice against federal courts, which are as much the courts of the whole people as the courts of the counties or of the circuits in a state." He ruled that the Arkansas legislature, in leaving the counties with the power to enter into contracts with citizens of other states, had "creat[ed] thereby a property right in favor of such citizens," which left the citizens with the right to sue in federal courts.

In an earlier case (*National Bank of Western Arkansas* v. *Sebastian County*) involving the same legislation of 1879, Parker ruled that the State of Arkansas had no authority to limit federal judicial power. Sebastian County had issued warrants promising to pay the holders. When payment was not forthcoming, the bank sued. While the case was pending in Parker's court, the legislature took away the power of a county to sue or be sued; "in other words," wrote Parker, the new law revoked "the sueable character of the counties." Earlier Arkansas legislation had declared a county to be "a body corporate and politic," which could sue and be sued "in *any* court." Parker believed the Arkansas law of 1879 had been passed to prevent holders of the warrants from bringing suit against the counties in the federal courts. He ruled that states could neither enlarge nor diminish the jurisdiction of the federal courts. Moreover, the warrants were contracts and as such were protected by the contract clause of the United States Constitution (Article X, section 1). Since the Arkansas statute of 1879 "impaired the obligation of a contract," it was, in Parker's view, void.

Corporations did not always fare badly before Parker's tribunal. For example, in one case Robert Crawson sued the Western Union Telegraph Company for its failure to deliver a

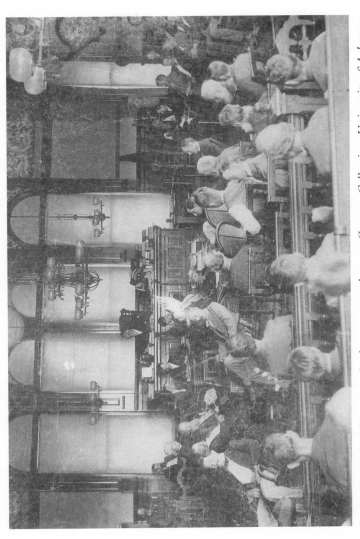

Judge Parker holding court in the new courthouse. *Cravens Collection, University of Arkansas at Little Rock Archives.*

message on time. His brother-in-law had sent him a telegram urging him to "come on this evening train. Ma wants to see you." ("Ma" was Crawson's mother-in-law, who was apparently dying.) Crawson claimed that the company's delay in getting the message to him caused suffering, which entitled him to damages. Parker ruled against Crawson. He held that mental suffering, unaccompanied by physical suffering, did not entitle the plaintiff to an award. He correctly interpreted the law of tort of that period, which required a physical manifestation of emotional distress in order to recover damages. Moreover, the company's failure to deliver the telegram was "ordinary willful negligence" and did not "indicate wantonness or malicious purpose."

The Liggett and Myer Tobacco Company was another major business concern that had reason to be pleased with a decision by Parker. The company charged that the trademark of a rival manufacturer of plug tobacco too closely resembled theirs. Examining the two trademarks, the judge observed that they were not identical and that the differences between them "would, perhaps, be at once detected by the intelligent user of tobacco, looking for his favorite brand, just as the man of luxurious tastes would discern his favorite brand of champagne." Nevertheless, the similarities were capable of deceiving the "ordinary purchaser." Parker decided in favor of Liggett and Myer. Here again he ruled in accordance with the common law, which stated that if an "ordinary" consumer could not readily detect differences between trademarks, the user of the infringing trademark was "poaching," and, in this case, causing Liggett and Myer to suffer damage because of diversion of sales or the dilution of the significance of their trademark.

As in the criminal cases brought before him, it was uncommon for Parker to decide that his court lacked jurisdiction, but there were instances when he was compelled to dismiss cases on that ground. At issue in *Culver et al. v. County of Crawford* (1877) was a federal law that said that the matter in dispute had to exceed five hundred dollars for a federal circuit court to have jurisdiction. The county of Crawford argued that the case involved less than that sum. Judge Parker agreed, stating that the court must look to the amount stated in the body of the complaint, not the amount alleged by the plaintiff. Parker sustained the defendant's motion to dismiss.

More in keeping with Parker's usual inclination to assert jurisdiction was his ruling in *Culver* v. *Woodruff County* (1878). An act of Congress in the previous year had taken counties out of the Western District of Arkansas and put them in the Eastern District. He held that any cases pending in his court involving residents of those counties should remain in his court.

In another case, *Connor* v. *Scott* (1876), the defendant sought to remove the case from an Arkansas state circuit court to the United States District Court for the Western District of Arkansas. Parker determined that this request was correct because the case called for an interpretation of the federal bankruptcy laws. He quoted Chief Justice John Marshall to support his position: "[W]e have no more right to decline the exercise of jurisdiction which is given than to usurp that which is not given; the one or the other would be treason to the constitution."

In *Bland and others* v. *Fleeman and others* (1887), which included an accusation of fraud against the administrator of an estate, Parker reluctantly dismissed the case for lack of jurisdiction. He was convinced that the parties had "arrang[ed] themselves as plaintiffs or defendants," the result being "a collusive joinder of parties to confer jurisdiction" on the circuit court. "It is usurpation for a court to take jurisdiction where it does not have it under the law." He rejected the case "with some degree of regret" because "from the examination of the facts . . . I am led to the conclusion that the acts [of the administrator] bristle with fraud."

Others accused of questionable practices were not so fortunate. In *United States* v. *Culver et al.* (1892) Parker agreed with the government's contention that defendants had fraudulently bought federal lands in Arkansas, claiming that they were agricultural lands, all the while knowing that they were non-purchasable mineral lands. Parker voided the patent.

Believing that parts of a mortgage contract were harsh and unjust, Parker, in *Tilley et ux.* v. *American Building & Loan Association* (1892), canceled that section of the contract containing the objectionable terms. In that same year, however, in *Dryfus* v. *Burnes et ux.*, he rejected the defendant's accusation of usury, holding that the bonus paid to the agent, Dryfus, to get the loan was not part of the sum paid for it.

At least once during his tenure on the federal bench, Parker was sent by the judge of the Eighth Circuit to hear cases in Colorado. The regular judge of the district, Moses Hallett, was presumably incapacitated or on leave. One of the cases Parker heard no doubt captured the attention of many citizens of the state. *Daniels* v. *Benedict et al.* (1892) was a proceeding in which the wife of a wealthy citizen of Denver contested a divorce granted by a county court. Lilyan Daniels claimed that her husband, William, had forced her from their home and refused to support her. She then moved to Cheyenne, Wyoming, and later to Chicago and New York City. She alleged that she had become ill in mind and body and that while she was debilitated and destitute, agents of her husband, pretending to be sympathetic, urged her to accept a divorce. They assured her, she claimed, that it would be based only on the grounds of abandonment and desertion. After agreeing to this, she later learned that William Daniels had obtained the divorce in the court for Arapahoe County, Colorado, on the grounds of adultery. Meanwhile, he died, having left her out of his will. Mrs. Daniels brought suit in the United States Circuit Court for the District of Colorado, Judge Isaac C. Parker presiding. She sought an annulment of the decree of divorce on the grounds of fraud, denied that she was an adulteress, and argued that she was entitled to one-half of her deceased husband's property. She also claimed that the court of Arapahoe County did not have jurisdiction to hear and decide a divorce case.

Parker expressed his belief that the woman was partly to blame, but less so than the other parties. A court of equity, he stated, will "aid the one who is comparatively the more innocent." Accordingly, he overruled the legatees of the will, who were the defendants in the case. He declined to go further with the case, however, because he believed that he was not capable of ruling on the important matter of the powers of the county court: "It is a question of such delicacy, and one which may be so far-reaching in its effects, that I prefer that it should be settled, if to be settled at all, by my brother Hallett." The Colorado jurist was "more familiar with the [state's] constitution and laws than I am." When Hallett resumed his duties, he dismissed the case and ordered Mrs. Daniels to pay the defendants twenty-five dollars in restitution for their legal fees.

As a judge presiding over civil controversies, Parker heard and decided cases embracing a wide variety of concerns. Most were important only to the parties immediately involved. Others, such as those affecting the status of the Indian nations, were farther reaching. In general, he showed a desire to protect Indian rights, but found that he had to rule against them when notions of tribal sovereignty clashed with federal authority.

There is no clear indication that Parker was biased for or against business interests. It is obvious, however, that in personal injury suits brought against the railroads, he was much inclined to favor those seeking damages. Also apparent is his usual determination to resist challenges to his court's jurisdiction.

In the last years of Parker's tenure, his decisions and the verdicts of his juries in civil cases were subject to appeal. In some instances, the higher courts reversed him. When they did, surely he was not pleased, but he refrained from publicly criticizing the judges who overruled him. He was to show no such restraint when confronted with the many reversals handed down by the United States Supreme Court in criminal cases.

CHAPTER 6

In the Interest of Humanity

FROM its inception in 1851, the United States District Court for the Western District of Arkansas had exercised circuit court powers without having a separate circuit court. The federal judges of the districts of western South Carolina and northern Mississippi likewise had circuit court powers but were without circuit courts. In 1888, Senator James K. Jones of Arkansas introduced a bill to eliminate the circuit court powers of these tribunals and provide them with circuit courts. Proponents of the bill said the changes would bring about a greater degree of uniformity within the federal court system. For the court at Fort Smith, the proposed overhaul of its jurisdiction meant that the judge of the Eighth Circuit and the Supreme Court justice assigned to the circuit could hear cases there, including appeals from the district court. The most significant part of the bill was a section that allowed appeals to the Supreme Court of death sentences handed down in all federal courts. Specifically addressing the situation in the Western District of Arkansas, where the vast majority of federal capital cases were tried, Senator Jones said that "the commonest principles of humanity" demanded that "this anomaly in our judicial system" be changed to provide a "remedy for what seems to be an outrageous wrong."

Senator George G. Vest, Parker's outspoken critic, voiced his support for these changes. Vest declared that "for years men have been executed without any right to ask the judgment of the Supreme Court of the United States whether it be judicial murder or not." A substitute bill, drafted by Senator George Hoar of Massachusetts, passed the Senate. In the lower house, Representative John H. Rogers, who was a resident of Fort Smith, urged passage of the measure. It was, he said, "a burning shame" that those convicted of capital crimes in federal courts had no access to a higher court. Rogers noted that in his own city "there are some forty persons confined in jail subject to trial at the session of the court just begun, and I am anxious that this right shall be guaranteed to those unfortunate persons." The bill before the lawmakers was "in the interest of humanity," Rogers said. Approved by both houses of the Congress, the act went to President Grover Cleveland, who killed it with a pocket veto because he had confidence in Parker.

The next session of the Congress saw the introduction of a practically identical bill. With minor amendments, it passed both houses and, on February 6, 1889, became law without Cleveland's signature. It abolished the circuit court powers of the District Courts of Western Arkansas, Western South Carolina, and Northern Mississippi, and established circuit courts for each. Marshals and district attorneys of the district courts were to function also as the marshals and attorneys for the circuit courts. The law authorized the judges to appoint a separate clerk for each of the tribunals, but Parker apparently chose to have his long-time colleague Stephen Wheeler act as clerk for both. As noted earlier, the circuit courts exercised mostly original jurisdiction and had only limited appellate jurisdiction.

Of greatest significance to Parker was Section 6 of the statute. It authorized the Supreme Court to examine, reverse, or affirm any capital case brought before it on a writ of error directed to a lower federal court. While the appeal was pending, the writ was to "operate as a stay of proceedings upon the judgment in respect of which it is sued out." The long overdue provision for appeals of capital cases reflects a movement toward more leniency in criminal jurisprudence and was not necessarily a reaction to what was seen as Parker's harshness. Nevertheless, the court at Fort Smith was obviously the main object of Section 6.

The nation's legal press generally supported the change. The *American Law Review* was pleased to report that there was no longer "the great outrage of denying the right of appeal in a capital case while granting it in a case involving $5,000 worth of property." Parker himself, in the midst of his clashes with the Supreme Court, claimed to have no objection to the right of appeal.

Over the next few years, the Supreme Court was to hand down an astonishingly large number of reversals of Fort Smith murder convictions. The overturning of his court's criminal convictions infuriated Parker. Already noted were the Supreme Court's reversals of the convictions of John Boyd, Robert M. Hall, Mary Kettenring, Ely Lucas, Charles Smith, and Eugene Standley. In non-capital cases, the Supreme Court had reversed the decision in the Sarlls beer case and granted a writ of habeas corpus for accused adulterer John Mayfield.

From 1891 until 1897, forty-four death penalty cases were appealed from Parker's court—some of them two and three times. The Supreme Court upheld twelve of the convictions, but found reversible error in thirty of the cases and remanded them to the lower court for retrial. In the new trials, sixteen of the defendants were acquitted or discharged. Of the remainder, seven were convicted of manslaughter. Another seven were again found guilty of murder. Six of the latter appealed again to Supreme Court and again secured reversals. One condemned man died before he could be executed. Some of the men sentenced to death on retrial received commutations from the president, and one was sent to an insane asylum. In 1893 alone, appeals of criminal cases from the Western District of Arkansas accounted for four percent of the caseload of an already overburdened Supreme Court.

Former Attorney General Augustus H. Garland, now in private practice in Washington, D.C., represented several of those who took their case from Parker's circuit court to the Supreme Court on appeal, usually with success. His son, R. C. Garland, sometimes appeared as co-counsel. Also frequently arguing on behalf of the appellants was William M. Cravens. Others who appeared as counsel for the plaintiffs in error included Benjamin Du Val, Jacob C. Hodge, S. B. Maxey, Ira D. Oglesby, J. Warren Reed, and John H. Rogers. Among those who represented the defendant in error, the United States, were Assistant Attorneys General Holmes Conrad, J. M. Dickinson, and Edward B. Whitney. Later, Conrad became solicitor general and represented the government in some of the cases appealed from Fort Smith, as did his successor, Lawrence Maxwell, Jr. Sometimes the government attorneys lost even when the appellants were not represented by counsel.

The grounds for the reversals were many and varied, but mostly they involved Judge Parker's instructions to the juries. Often the justices found Parker's wording calculated to incline the jurors toward a guilty verdict. Before the Civil War, judges commonly let juries know what verdicts they expected of them; later in the century this practice was no longer acceptable, but Parker continued the older style of charging a jury. Some reversals were based on Parker's allowing the prosecutor to use provocative rhetoric. Several of the convictions were overturned because the Supreme Court found error in Parker's distinctions between murder and manslaughter. Related to the question of defining the two types of homicide was the issue of self-defense, another area in which the justices and the judge differed. Parker's lengthy instructions to juries—some ranging from forty to seventy typewritten pages—contained much that was confusing and contradictory. Reading the opinions handed down by the Supreme Court reversing the Parker court, one cannot help suspecting that the justices' obligatory references to "the learned judge" were heavy with sarcasm.

The act permitting Supreme Court review of capital cases became effective on May 1, 1889. Not until Parker had ordered the execution of ten men, however, did someone take advantage of the right to appeal. The first was William Alexander, who had been accused of murdering David C.

Steadman, his partner in a horse-selling venture, in the Creek Nation. Before Steadman's decomposed corpse was discovered, Alexander had consulted with a Muskogee lawyer, J. G. Ralls (or Rawles), telling him that Steadman had run off with a married woman and left him with the horses they had obtained in Arizona. Without actually hiring Ralls, Alexander had asked his opinion about the ownership of the horses. The attorney testified at Alexander's trial before Parker, at which he was found guilty. In an opinion for a unanimous Supreme Court delivered by Justice Henry B. Brown, the justices ruled that the communication between Alexander and Ralls was "plainly privileged" and should not have been admitted as testimony. There were two retrials, and in each Parker took pains to ensure that they were fair to the accused man. In both, the jury was unable to reach a verdict, and Alexander was set free when the prosecution declined to press for another trial.

There was little unhappiness in the Indian Territory over the Supreme Court's decision and Alexander's subsequent release because many thought he was innocent. Usually, the press and people within Parker's jurisdiction, particularly in Fort Smith, sided with their judge in his troubles with the Court. For instance, in 1892, when the *Saint Louis Republic* criticized Parker for his harshness in murder cases, the *Fort Smith Elevator* rushed to his defense: "If the *Republic* could see and understand the class of criminals with which Judge Parker has to deal, we doubt not that its opinions would undergo a material change."

At issue in *Collins* v. *United States* (1893) was the question of murder or manslaughter. The defendant, a youth of eighteen, killed a man who had assaulted his twelve-year-old brother at a dance. Parker had told the jury that passion alone could not reduce the charge to manslaughter. To be justifiable, passion must "generate from some wrongful act being done by the party who is slain at the time that he does it, or so soon thereafter as that there was not time for the passion of the party to cool." The jury found for murder. Speaking through Justice David J. Brewer, the Supreme Court found no fault with Parker's interpretation and let the conviction stand. Because of his youth and Parker's intercession, Frank Collins received a commutation to life imprisonment.

Another defendant, John Brown, was thrice convicted of murdering two deputy marshals and each time won a reversal. The first reversal occurred because Parker had admitted testimony alleging a conspiracy and told the jury that "the declarations of a party or parties as to their participation in the criminal act were competent evidence of the conspiracy." Brown appealed his second conviction and again succeeded in getting the verdict set aside. Parker had erred, said Justice John Marshall Harlan, when he told the jury that "the verdict of guilty of murder or manslaughter turns alone upon an inquiry as to the way in which the killing was done." The third trial resulted in another guilty verdict. The third reversal prompted Justice Brewer to write a biting dissent, which Justices Henry B. Brown and Rufus Peckham joined. Their brethren on the Supreme Court found Parker's instructions regarding the reputation of a witness "too narrow and restrictive." Brewer pointed out that in three trials, thirty-six men had found Brown guilty of murder. "Justice and the protection of society unite in saying that it is high time such a crime was punished." As for the reputation of a witness, Brewer added, it "is the general judgment of the community in respect to the witness whose reputation is challenged, and is not made up by the flippant talk of a few outlaws." At Brown's fourth trial, which took place after Parker's death, he was sentenced to one year in prison.

Another person convicted three times for murder was Alexander Allen, a fourteen-year-old black youth accused of fatally shooting an eighteen-year-old white youth who, with others, had attacked Allen with sticks. On Allen's first appeal, the Supreme Court, speaking through Chief Justice Fuller, concluded that Parker's instructions to the jury regarding self-defense and justifiable homicide were erroneous because he had substituted "abstract conceptions for the actual facts of the particular case as they appeared to the defendant at the time." Brewer, joined by Brown, disagreed, arguing that the majority based its opinion on some of Parker's introductory remarks rather than his actual instructions as to the law. Found guilty on retrial, Allen again appealed. This time the Supreme Court, speaking through Justice George Shiras, faulted Parker for excluding virtually any consideration of self-defense and for telling the jurors that the defendant's intentional arming of himself meant that they could only find for murder or manslaughter. A third trial, a third conviction, and a third appeal followed. In the final hearing of *Allen* v. *United States*, the Supreme Court affirmed the lower court's guilty verdict, finding nothing objectionable in the judge's instructions. Allen was spared the gallows when President Cleveland commuted the sentence to life, based on the recommendation of members of the Supreme Court and the statement of the district attorney "to the effect that the extreme penalty of the law should not be inflicted upon him." Allen's age was no doubt a factor.

In another case, Sam Hickory, a Cherokee man, had been found guilty of murdering a deputy marshal. The Supreme Court reversed the verdict and granted a new trial because, in an opinion delivered by Chief Justice Melville W. Fuller, Parker's instructions relating to premeditation were erroneous. A second trial brought another guilty verdict. Hickory's second appeal secured another reversal. Justice Edward White's opinion for a unanimous Court chastised Parker for his misinterpretations of concealment and flight. Parker had cited the biblical account of Cain and Abel on the subject of concealment of crime. White acknowledged that acts of concealment were competent to go to the jury, "yet they are not to be considered alone as conclusive, or as creating a legal presumption of guilt." Parker's charge to the jury on this point had been "plainly erroneous": "It magnified and distorted the proving power of the facts of concealment." Likewise, Parker had quoted the Bible regarding flight ("The wicked flee when no man pursueth"). These and other of the judge's remarks about flight were, in White's words, "tantamount to saying . . . that flight created a legal presumption of guilt, so strong and so conclusive, that it was the duty of the jury to act on it as an axiomatic truth." Other instructions by Parker were "clearly illegal." The justice summed up the Court's objections in strong words: "The charge given in this case violates every rule thus announced. It was neither calm nor impartial. It put every deduction that could be drawn against the accused from the proof of concealment and flight and omitted or obscured the converse aspect." The result of Hickory's third trial was a five-year prison sentence.

The High Court also overturned the conviction of John Gourko, a Polish coal miner accused of killing a fellow miner in the Choctaw Nation. Speaking through John Marshall Harlan, the justices found that Parker's long charge to the jury was "wanting in the clearness that was requisite in order that the jury might not misapprehend the principles of law by which they were to be controlled." In particular, the Court objected to the judge's interpretations of what constituted murder, manslaughter, and self-defense. At the retrial Gourko pleaded guilty to manslaughter and drew a four-year sentence in the Columbus, Ohio, penitentiary.

In yet another case, *Thompson* v. *United States*, The Supreme Court reversed the Fort Smith court because Parker's jury charge had been "prolix, confusing, abstract, argumentative, and misleading," particularly as it related to self-defense. The instructions of the "learned judge," wrote Justice Shiras, were "not easy to understand," and he "seem[ed] to confuse" some of the facts of the case. In both the Gourko and Thompson cases, the Court said Parker had been wrong in letting the jury think that the defendants' arming of themselves "showed a purpose to kill formed before the actual affray."

Self-defense was again the main issue in *Allison* v. *United States*. In this case, John Allison claimed he had killed his father for making violent threats against him. Parker told the jury that the defendant's word alone was not enough to establish self-defense. The Supreme Court found that Parker's instructions downplayed the father's threats and tended to make the jury think that Allison had "hunted up" the victim. Chief Justice Fuller concluded with: "Where the charge of the trial judge takes the form of animated argument, the liability is great that the propositions of the law may become interrupted by digression, and so intermingled with inferences springing from forensic ardor, that the jury are left without proper instructions." Allison's new trial resulted in a sentence of seven years' imprisonment.

Clearly, the Supreme Court and Isaac Parker were in disagreement over what constituted self-defense. They also held different views on the related matter of the duty to retreat. We have seen that Parker stood by the old rule that a person, when threatened, must use every means, including flight, to avoid bloodshed. Other courts, including the nation's highest, were moving toward acceptance of "no duty to retreat." Justice Harlan in particular adopted the newer view.

Not all of the reversals involving self-defense were murder cases. For example, Babe Beard was convicted of manslaughter and sentenced by Parker to eight years' imprisonment. Will Jones, armed and accompanied by his two brothers, had entered Beard's property and threatened to kill Beard because he had a cow they claimed was theirs. Beard crushed Jones's skull with a shotgun. In reversing the verdict, Justice Harlan's opinion stated that Beard had the right to stand his ground and that Parker was wrong to tell the jury there was a duty to retreat.

In another case, David Cul Rowe, a Cherokee, had been indicted for killing a white man who had told Rowe that he had "got too damn much nigger blood in him to talk anything with any sense" and had attacked Rowe with a knife. Rowe appealed his five-year sentence for manslaughter. Once more, Harlan expressed his adamant opposition to Parker's views on self-defense and the duty to retreat—which the Arkansas judge had spelled out in a twenty-seven-page jury charge. Harlan stated bluntly that the parts of the charge to which the defense had objected "were well calculated to mislead the jury." Did the law, the justice asked, "require that the accused should stand still, and permit himself to be cut to pieces, under the penalty that if he met an unlawful attack upon him and saved his own life, by taking that of his assailant, he would be guilty of manslaughter? We think not."

On similar grounds, the Supreme Court, reversed the murder conviction of Ed Alberty, a black man. He had killed another black man who was trying to enter Alberty's wife's room through a window and who, when discovered, had threatened Alberty with a knife. On the jurisdictional question, the Court agreed that the case had been properly before the Fort Smith court because Alberty was a "member of the Cherokee Nation, but not an Indian," and that the man he had killed was "a colored citizen of the United States." The reversal was based on Parker's instructions to the jury regarding the duty to retreat and the attempt to disarm the intruder, which were held to be "misleading." Again Parker had quoted the biblical passage about the wicked fleeing, which Brown, using White's language in the *Hickory* opinion, said was "tantamount to saying to the jury that flight created a legal presumption of guilt so strong and conclusive that it was the duty of the jury to act on it as an axiomatic truth." The jury acquitted Alberty at his second trial.

The most notorious beneficiary of a Supreme Court reversal of Parker's court was Henry Starr, a young part-Cherokee outlaw related by marriage to Belle Starr. He came before Parker charged with murdering Floyd Wilson, a member of a deputy marshal's posse. Starr's autobiography records that Parker's instructions to the jury took two hours and forty minutes and "for legal pomposity and hazy insinuations, it would rank high." The jury found Starr guilty after deliberating, according to Starr, for only a half an hour. Following the pronouncement of the death sentence, Parker delivered a twenty-minute lecture to the condemned man, "but," Starr wrote, "he failed in his object. That fellow never could scare me." Starr also claimed that the judge, whom he called the "Nero of America," "to show his appreciation, ordered that the jury be given supper at the government's expense." The young outlaw believed that Parker "was no doubt an able man, and of extensive legal learning," but that he had been struggling with lawbreakers for so long "that his mind was warped on that particular subject, and those closest to him admitted that he was a Monmoniac [sic] on the subject of crime." It was while awaiting trial that Starr had convinced his fellow inmate, Crawford Goldsby, "Cherokee Bill," of the futility of his attempted jailbreak.

When Starr's case was appealed to the Supreme Court, Chief Justice Fuller found much to criticize in Parker's jury charge. The judge's interpretation of self-defense was again held to be erroneous and his language "tended fatally to mislead." Fuller's opinion noted that it was not certain that the victim had clearly identified himself as an officer of the law before he began shooting at Starr. Parker had pointed out to the jury that, at the time of the killing, Starr was a fugitive from justice, having jumped his bail bond on a larceny charge. To this, Fuller responded that a man need not be pure of heart to kill in self-defense; nor should his occupation, previous conduct, or location have any bearing. The chief justice stated that Parker's instructions mixed law and facts, the latter being the province of the jury only. He found fault, too, with Parker's statements to the jury about the Indian Territory being a "Golgotha to [law] officers." Fuller quoted other passionate, argumentative, and sarcastic remarks by Parker, including the following: "What was this posse to do? What was [Wilson] commanded to do? To go into the Indian country and hunt up Mr. Starr, and say to him that on a certain day the judge of the Federal court at Fort Smith will want your attendance at a little trial down there wherein you are charged with horsestealing, and you will be kind enough, sir, to put in your attendance on that day; and the judge sends his compliments to you, Mr. Starr."

Fuller wrote that "The circumstances of this case apparently aroused the indignation of the learned judge in an uncommon degree." Nevertheless, he added, "that indignation was expressed in terms which were not consistent with the due regard to the right of the jury to exercise an independent judgment or with the circumspection and caution which should characterize judicial utterances." The chief justice concluded by expressing the Court's "disapprobation of this mode of instructing and advising a jury." Reversed and remanded with a direction to grant a new trial, Henry Starr's case went back to Fort Smith.

The retrial resulted in another guilty verdict. Starr appealed the second conviction and got another reversal. Justice White, speaking for the Court, brushed aside objections that the arrest warrant was defective because it was not in "due form." White did find, however, that Starr's attorneys raised other points of merit, notably Parker's erroneous implication that flight was evidence of guilt. The opinion excused the judge by saying that the "error committed by the court doubtless resulted from the fact that the case was tried before the ruling in either the *Hickory* or *Alberty* case was announced."

Years later, America's foremost early twentieth-century authority on evidence, John H. Wigmore, supported Parker's view on flight as a presumption of guilt and expressed the belief that the Supreme Court's decisions in *Hickory*, *Alberty*, and *Starr* were "ill-advised" and had an "unfortunate influence" on other cases.

At his third trial, conducted after Parker's death, Starr was allowed to plead guilty to manslaughter and was sent to the Columbus, Ohio, prison for five years. President Theodore Roosevelt issued a pardon in 1903, based on Starr's role in the surrender of his fellow inmate Crawford Goldsby. Starr resumed his outlaw life and was imprisoned in 1909 for robbing a Colorado bank. Again he was pardoned, only to return to his old ways, and he was shot and captured while leading a double bank robbery in Stroud, Oklahoma. Once more he received clemency, gaining first parole and later a pardon. In 1921, soon after playing himself in a film based on his life, Henry Starr was killed while robbing a bank in Harrison, Arkansas.

Even Justice Brewer, Parker's most dependable Supreme Court ally, did not always support Parker. Brewer wrote the Court's opinion reversing the convictions of brothers Jess and John Nofire, Cherokees convicted of the murder of a white man who had married a Cherokee. Parker had told the jury that because evidence of the murdered man's Cherokee citizenship was insufficient, the case was properly in his court, not a Cherokee tribunal. A major consideration was the fact that neither the clerk of the Tahlequah District nor his deputy had signed the victim's marriage license. Brewer, however, said that the person who signed the license, the deputy's son, was the de facto deputy and therefore authorized to sign. This and other proof of the murdered man's citizenship led the Court to the conclusion that the Nofire brothers had killed an adopted member of the tribe. Accordingly, the decision remanded the case with instructions to surrender the defendants to the Cherokee authorities.

The case of Famous Smith likewise presented a jurisdictional question. Smith, a Cherokee, was convicted of killing a white man. On appeal, his attorney argued that the deceased was a Cherokee citizen and that the matter properly belonged in a Cherokee court. The Supreme Court, speaking through Justice Brown, agreed, holding that the burden of proving that the victim was a white man was on the prosecution, and that "the testimony offered by the government had no legitimate tendency to prove that the murdered man was not an Indian." The case went back to Fort Smith, where the district attorney declined to initiate a second trial, entering a nolle prosequi.

Parker's definition of the crime of rape—specifically, whether force was required to commit the act, or simply nonconsent of the woman—was the basis of an appeal in *Mills* v. *United States*. Speaking for his Supreme Court colleagues, Justice Peckham believed that the trial judge had defined it correctly at one point in his instructions to the jury but had explained it incorrectly elsewhere. The erroneous version "may have found lodgment in the minds of the jury." Also, the evidence of the commission of the crime, said Peckham, "impresses us as being unsatisfactory." At the retrial of James Mills, the jury could not agree; a third trial ended with an acquittal. Curiously, the defendant, according to the alleged victim's husband, had identified himself as "Henry Starr."

In a murder case reversed by the Supreme Court, Frank Carver, jealous of another man, had fatally wounded his mistress, Anna Maledon, the daughter of hangman George Maledon. Carver's brain was addled at the time by heavy drinking of Jamaica ginger and hard cider. In an opinion delivered by Chief Justice Fuller, the Court reversed Carver's conviction "upon the ground that improper evidence had been received of an alleged dying declaration." Another conviction and another appeal followed. In the second Carver case brought to the High Court, disagreement among witnesses concerning Anna's deathbed statement was again at issue. After noting that dying declarations were not always reliable and truthful and could not be given the same weight as sworn testimony, Justice Brown set the conviction aside and ordered a new trial. Carver's third trial took place after Parker's death, and the jury exercised the new option and chose life imprisonment instead of hanging. George Maledon was thereby denied any satisfaction he might have gained from seeing his daughter's killer hanged.

In *Lewis* v. *United States*, the Court, speaking through Justice Shiras, ruled that Parker had committed an error "in directing secret challenges [of prospective jurors] to be made, and not in the presence of the prisoner and the jurors." Brewer, joined by Brown, dissented, arguing that the court journal showed that the defendant "was in fact present" during the challenging. Alexander Lewis was retried at Fort Smith and acquitted.

One of several issues in the case of John Hicks was the abetting and encouraging of a crime. Officers killed Stand Rowe while attempting to arrest him for murder. Hicks, an accomplice, was accused of having abetted and encouraged Rowe to commit the crime. Hicks was found guilty of murder and appealed. The Supreme Court's opinion, delivered by Shiras, found much that was wrong with the proceedings at Fort Smith: Parker's charge failed to instruct the jury on *intent* to abet and encourage; no facts were presented to show that the encounter between the murdered man and Rowe had been the result of a conspiracy; Parker had told the jury that the testimony of other witnesses outweighed that of the accused because they were "telling the truth"; he had further informed the jury that they should take into account the defendant's interest in the case when considering his testimony. Brewer and Brown again dissented. They saw no error in Parker's instructions and asserted that abetting a crime implied intent to do so. Hicks gained an acquittal at his second trial.

John Graves was also acquitted on retrial. He appealed the murder conviction of his first trial and won a reversal because Parker, in the view of the Supreme Court, should have stopped the district attorney from commenting on the absence of the defendant's wife at the trial. "It was," said Justice Brown, "as if the court had charged the jury that it was a circumstance against [Graves] that he had failed to produce his wife in court."

The case of Dennis Davis involved the always difficult question of the sanity of someone accused of murder. Davis was found guilty of killing Sol Blackwell in the Creek Nation. At the trial, witnesses stated that Davis was "half crazy [and] weak-minded." In what was described as an "elaborate" charge, Parker had told the jury that the law assumed everyone to be sane unless insanity could be proved, and that the burden of proof fell upon the defendant. Speaking for a unanimous Court, Justice Harlan cited many American and English authorities on the vexing problem of sanity in criminal proceedings. His opinion held that a jury could not find a defendant guilty of murder if the evidence "is equally balanced on the issue as to the sanity of the accused at the time of the killing." The case showed that there was considerable disagreement in legal circles over the insanity plea. There was, however, no disagreement among the justices in this case, and they ordered a new trial. At the second trial Davis was again found guilty and again he appealed. Insanity was once more the central question, but this time there was much discussion of expert testimony, which at Davis's retrial was given by a medical doctor. A unanimous Supreme Court, through an opinion by Brewer, ruled that a judge must be allowed discretion to limit such testimony. Davis, in later proceedings, was judged insane and ended his days in an asylum rather than at the end of a noose.

Parker had reason to believe that the Department of Justice sometimes contributed to his difficulties in cases that were appealed to the Supreme Court. The Court overturned the convictions of Buz Luckey, Thomas J. Thornton, and James Dyer "upon confession of error" by the government attorneys, a plea admitting to the appellants' assignment of errors. In other words, they believed it was futile to contest the appeal. On retrial, Luckey was acquitted but later drew a fifteen-year sentence for train robbery. Thornton's second trial resulted in a ten-year sentence at the Columbus, Ohio, prison.

The satisfaction Parker may have felt when the High Court upheld his court's guilty verdicts in capital cases is not known. Given the much larger number of reversals, it was probably small comfort to him when the Court occasionally affirmed the results of trials at Fort Smith. Already mentioned was the upholding of the convictions of Crawford Goldsby ("Cherokee Bill"), members of the Buck gang, Johnny Pointer, James C. Casharego ("George W. Wilson"), and Mollie King. Others whose convictions were upheld were Bood Crumpton, Webber Isaacs, George and John Pierce (or Pearce), Willie Johnson (alias Overton), Lewis Holder, Marshal Tucker, and Edward Wilkey.

The Court, in the opinion by Justice Brown, ruled in Crumpton's case that the defense attorney's exceptions made at the trial were not reviewable. The Crumpton case was the first appeal of a murder conviction in Parker's court that the Supreme Court upheld. The *American Law Review* (July–August 1891) took the decision as a sign that the justices would not reverse the Arkansas court on the minor technicalities that characterized appeals in the state courts: "errors of equal dignity with the question of whether the clerk licked the seal with his tongue or moistened it with a sponge."

Brown's opinion in the Isaacs case held that Parker had correctly overruled a motion for a continuance. Further, the Fort Smith court had jurisdiction, the accused being a Cherokee and the deceased a white man. Finally, it was not reversible error if Parker had omitted to give instructions not requested by the defendant: "It is sufficient that the court give no erroneous instructions."

One of many points raised in the appeals of the Pierce brothers was the admissibility of confessions given by the accused while in custody. It was sufficient, the Supreme Court ruled, that the confessions were "not extorted by inducements or threats."

At issue in the appeal of Willie Johnson were the "constructive, as distinguished from actual, presence at the scene of the murder," the need to prove motive, and the weight attached to the defendant's testimony on his own behalf. The Court, speaking through Brewer, had no problems with upholding the lower court on these points. The justices agreed that there was room for reasonable doubt of Johnson's guilt, but held that Parker's overruling of a motion for a new trial showed that he was satisfied with the verdict. At his second trial, Johnson was sent to prison for life.

During the testimony of a witness at the trial of Lewis Holder, Parker had ordered all other witnesses from the courtroom. Holder's attorney objected when he saw that one of them had remained. In the opinion by Justice Fuller, the Supreme Court saw no error in allowing this witness to testify even if he had disregarded the judge's order. Fuller also said that the objections to Parker's charge to the jury were too general to raise any questions for the Court to review.

The Supreme Court easily disposed of the appeal of Marshal Tucker, who had killed Lula May, a prostitute. At trial, Tucker claimed that he had been drunk and "entertained no malice" toward the victim. His appeal was based on an affidavit he had submitted requesting that certain witnesses be summoned and that the government pay their fees because he could not. His attorney objected to the introduction of the affidavit at the trial. He also objected to Parker's refusal to instruct the jury about drunkenness as a defense. Justice Gray's opinion found no merit in these points and affirmed the verdict. The justices had even less difficulty rejecting Edward Wilkey's appeal of conviction for rape, which they did with a terse memorandum opinion: "Judgment affirmed." Neither Tucker nor Wilkey was hanged. Upon the recommendations of Parker, the district attorney, and, in Wilkey's case, eleven jurors, both sentences were commuted to life imprisonment. Tucker's crime "seem[ed] to lack premeditation and deliberate intention"; Wilkey's was "a case where the death penalty ought not to be inflicted."

In a case involving the recurring problem of Indian citizenship, the Supreme Court upheld another of Parker's rulings. A "special Supreme Court of the Cherokee Nation" found Bob Talton guilty of murder. The convicted man filed for a writ of habeas corpus in the court for the Western District of Arkansas, alleging that, in violation of the laws and constitutions of the Cherokee Nation and the United States, he had been indicted by a grand jury of only five men and that there had been "gross irregularities" at his trial. Parker issued the writ, but after conducting a hearing he concluded that both Talton and the murdered man were Cherokees. He discharged the writ and remanded the prisoner to the custody of Wash Mayes, the high sheriff of the Cherokee Nation. Talton appealed to the Supreme Court, which, in an opinion by White, sustained Parker's action. The Court agreed that because Talton and his victim were both Indians, the case did not belong in a federal court; that the Fourteenth Amendment's requirement of due process of law did "not necessarily require an indictment by a grand jury in a prosecution by a state for murder"; and that the Fifth Amendment provision for grand jury indictments did not apply to a court of the Cherokee Nation, "whose powers of local self-government were enjoyed before the Constitution was made." A Cherokee court found Talton guilty and sentenced him to be hanged.

The Supreme Court also heard a few noncapital cases appealed from the Western District of Arkansas. In addition to the *Howell* Interstate Commerce Act case, there was a conviction for another nonviolent crime considered by the justices. Parker had sentenced Alexander W. Crain, a United States commissioner and pension notary in the Creek Nation, to three years at hard labor for filing a fraudulent Civil War pension claim. A divided Court reversed Parker. The six-man majority upheld the Fort Smith judge on all points raised by the plaintiff in error but one, which was the basis for a reversal: the trial record did not show that the accused had been formally arraigned; that, said Justice Harlan, amounted to a denial of due process of law. Although he acknowledged that Crain might be guilty, Harlan wrote that "it were better that he should escape altogether than that the court should sustain a judgment of conviction of an infamous crime where the record does not clearly show that there was a valid trial." The case was remanded so that the defendant could be properly arraigned and retried. Justice Peckham, with Brewer and White concurring, dissented: "I think such a result most deplorable." The majority, he wrote, had based its opinion on the "merest technicality" and an "unwarranted assumption of error." Peckham believed that it could be inferred from the facts that there had been an arraignment and a plea of not guilty and that it was reasonable to presume that the clerk of the lower court had simply failed to enter them into the record. The dissenting opinion also pointed out that the matter of the arraignment was raised for the first time by a "mere suggestion" at the end of counsel's brief for the Supreme Court.

Three convictions for assault with intent to kill came to the Supreme Court from Fort Smith. In *Acers* v. *United States*, Justice Brewer's opinion for the majority found no error in Parker's definition of a deadly weapon or in his instructions regarding self-defense, the presence of danger, and apparent danger. Brewer did, however, state that "It may be premised that the exceptions to [Parker's charge to the jury] are taken in the careless way which prevails in the western district of Arkansas." Parker died a few days after the decision, sparing him the pain Brewer's words might have caused, coming as they did from the man on the Court who had most often supported him.

Another assault case presented harder questions to the Supreme Court. George McElroy and five others were indicted for assault with intent to kill. One of the defendants was not brought to trial; the cases of the remaining five were consolidated and the accused were tried together and found guilty. Three of them were also indicted for and convicted of arson at the same trial. The Supreme Court, speaking through Chief Justice Fuller, held that "Such a joinder cannot be sustained where the parties are not the same, and where the offences are in nowise parts of the same transaction, and depend upon evidence of a different state of facts as to each or some of them." Assistant Attorney General Dickinson had conceded that the convictions of the two defendants who had not been indicted for arson, Thomas Stufflebeam and Charles Hook, should be reversed. The Court, however, reversed all five convictions.

Parker more directly and publicly clashed with the Supreme Court in another case involving assault with intent to kill. The defendant, Lafayette Hudson, was found guilty and sentenced to four years in prison. Hudson entered a motion for new trial, which Parker overruled, and Hudson then appealed to the Supreme Court. Before the clerk of the Fort Smith court issued a writ of error, Hudson applied to Justice White for a writ of error and a *supersedas* ordering a stay of proceedings, which was granted. White also permitted Hudson to furnish bond for five thousand dollars.

An indignant Parker responded by refusing to approve the bond or to discharge Hudson. He began his opinion by remarking, "this is one of the most important questions that ever presented itself to this court." He went on to claim that for twenty years, his court had "pursued the most liberal policy of any court in America on the subject of bail." Moreover, he stated that a trial court was in a better position to decide bail matters because it was more familiar than an appellate court with the character of the cases and of the defendants. Parker asserted that bail could only be admitted to accused persons before the trial, and he denied that the Supreme Court could authorize it after a conviction and pending an appeal. His main objection was that Justice White had no power to issue the writ because he was the Fifth Circuit Justice; the writ, said Parker, could come only from Brewer, the Eighth Circuit Justice (who had been absent from Washington when Hudson applied to the Court). He forcefully expressed the same views in a letter to Solicitor General Maxwell: "I refused to approve the bond because Mr. Justice White had no right to make the order and because the Supreme Court had no right to . . . [admit] parties to bail after conviction."

The matter then came before the Supreme Court as *Hudson* v. *Parker*, in which the petitioner, Hudson, sought a writ of mandamus, asking the Court to affirm White's order. In the meantime, Hudson was back in the Fort Smith jail, having been convicted, with others, of conspiring "to run away the principal witness against him."

Parker came to Washington to present his side personally in the mandamus case. Chief Justice Fuller refused to allow him to deliver an oral argument. Parker then attempted to have his brother-in-law and former law partner, Jefferson Chandler, now a noted Saint Louis attorney, present Parker's views instead of the solicitor general; this too met with failure. Parker and Solicitor General Maxwell submitted only briefs to the justices. Representing petitioner Hudson were William M. Cravens and Augustus H. Garland.

The Court, in an opinion by Justice Gray, ruled against Parker and issued the writ of mandamus, ordering Parker to admit Hudson to bail. Gray wrote that any justice had authority to issue the order Hudson sought and that there was no requirement that such an order had to come from the justice assigned to the circuit. In a dissenting opinion, concurred in by Justice Brown, Justice Brewer expressed his agreement with Parker's interpretation. Parker may have felt somewhat vindicated soon afterward when Hudson escaped from custody and remained at large.

During his stay in Washington, Parker took the opportunity to testify before the House Judiciary Committee. He argued unsuccessfully against a bill that would extinguish his court's jurisdiction and that of other outside courts in the Indian Territory. The night after his appearance before the committee, he dined with President Cleveland, but he failed to persuade the president to wait until the Indian Nations were better able to assume the responsibilities of citizenship before opening up the territory to settlement. Cleveland soon after signed into law the 1895 act that divided the Indian Territory into three federal judicial districts and eliminated the jurisdiction of the Arkansas, Kansas, and Texas courts in the territory. Since this last provision did not take effect until September 1, 1896, trials for crimes committed in the Indian Territory continued in Parker's court, as did appeals to the Supreme Court in Washington.

Several of the reversals of cases coming from Parker's court were based on the judge's inflammatory and argumentative rhetoric. The Supreme Court itself soon became the target of the judge's outbursts. At first he let his objections be known privately to officials in the Justice Department. In the process, he managed to offend the attorney general, the solicitor general, and their assistants—the very people who should have been his staunchest allies. In an 1893 letter he told the attorney general that "Many of these cases are very revolting murders and it is highly important that they should be thoroughly argued before the Supreme Court, as so far in cases of murder that have gone from this court, the court has reversed upon the merest technicalities." To have the cases "thoroughly argued," he wanted to send the complete transcript of

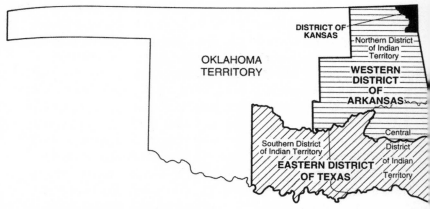

Federal Judicial Districts of Indian Territory, March 1, 1895 to August 31, 1896. Reproduced from Jeffrey Burton, *Indian Territory and the United States, 1866–1906: Courts, Government, and the Movement for Oklahoma Statehood* (Norman: University of Oklahoma Press, 1995, 219).

each case. The rules of the Supreme Court, however, required only summaries. The attorney general, caught in the middle, told the solicitor general that he wanted to follow the Supreme Court's wishes but did not want to offend Parker.

Parker also urged the Justice Department to act with greater speed in handling the appeals. Parker wrote that criminals who were out on bail pending their appeals to the Supreme Court were "tramping around, robbing people to get money to pay their lawyers with." The slow-moving machinery of justice encouraged "train robbers and desperadoes of all kinds . . . so that crime in the Indian Country is very largely on the increase." Delays in the appeals process, he told the government attorneys, destroyed the "effect of trial, conviction and punishment."

Adding to Parker's frustration in his losing battles with the Supreme Court were letters from criminals taunting him for his helplessness to prevent the reversals. He also received threatening letters that, he informed Solicitor General Maxwell, he paid "no attention to, although they are a little unpleasant and it is barely possible that there may be some danger behind them."

The arrival in Fort Smith of J. Warren Reed contributed further to Parker's inability to have justice done his way. Reed, a skillful and persuasive attorney, succeeded in getting "not guilty" verdicts for scores of clients standing trial in Parker's court. Many a criminal who would otherwise have been convicted found himself free thanks to Reed's considerable abilities. For clients found guilty, Reed prepared bills of exceptions, enumerating alleged errors committed in the trial court, which were the basis of several successful appeals.

Adding to Parker's sense of outrage was the news of Crawford Goldsby's escape attempt and his murder of guard Lawrence Keating, which reached the judge while visiting family in Saint Louis in July 1895. These events, along with his clashes with the Supreme Court, prompted Parker's passionate denunciation of the Court and the Justice

Department in an interview conducted by a reporter for the *Saint Louis Globe-Democrat.* Parker placed the responsibility for Keating's death squarely on the Court and the Justice Department. The latter had turned down his repeated requests for more guards, though his jail was "filled with murderers." He blamed the reversals handed down by the Supreme Court for the large number of desperate men incarcerated at Fort Smith and for the increase of crime generally. The Court's decisions had "contributed to the number of murders in the Indian Territory" because the appeals process gave the killers a "long breathing spell" between their conviction and the hearing of their cases before the Supreme Court. The overturning of the convictions was always "upon the flimsiest of technicalities," according to the irate judge.

Meanwhile, the reversals continued and efforts by the Justice Department to get the intractable Parker to change his ways were unavailing. Assistant Attorney General Edward B. Whitney wrote to Parker on January 29, 1896, advising him not to include in the transcripts sent to the Supreme Court those parts of the jury instructions that "are not assigned for error" in the plaintiff's bills of exceptions, because sometimes the Court found errors in the full transcripts that were not covered in the appellants' bills of exceptions. The suggestion only made Parker angrier, as did the Justice Department's confessions of error in the Luckey and Thornton cases. The Justice Department attorneys concluded that it was useless to argue either of the cases because Parker had failed to conduct the trials in accordance with the Supreme Court's previous rulings. Parker was further angered by what he believed was the Justice Department's inadequate handling of the appealed cases.

In an open letter to Attorney General Judson Harmon dated February 1896, published in the *Saint Louis Globe-Democrat*, Parker labeled Assistant Attorney General Whitney's confessions of error an "unprecedented and unwarranted action" that gave "security to criminals" and encouragement to "the man of blood." He also faulted the Justice Department attorneys for failing to argue appealed cases orally. In the same letter, he blasted the Supreme Court for its "vindictiveness against the trial court" and for misinterpreting, in his view, the law regarding self-defense and the duty to retreat. Parker charged that the members of the Supreme Court lacked experience in criminal law. Lending some validity to this last charge was the fact that Justice Brewer, who supported Parker's positions most often, had several years of service in the state courts of Kansas and ample experience in criminal matters.

Whitney wrote a spirited rebuttal in a letter to the *Saint Louis Republic* noting that the Justice Department had few problems getting the Supreme Court to sustain other federal courts. Parker, on the other hand, was "ignorant and careless with the law" and was reversed often because he refused to be guided by the Justice Department's instructions. Whitney conceded that the judge was well intentioned, but that he loaded his jury charges with "gross errors" in his zeal to convict. This was particularly deplorable, Whitney wrote, because many a guilty man escaped punishment because of Parker's wrong-headedness. Parker was "the best friend of the criminals" because of the reversals for which he was to blame.

Assistant Attorney General Whitney's letter provoked an abusive reply from Parker, this time in the pages of the *Fort Smith Weekly Elevator*. Whitney's letter in the *Republic* was, cried Parker, a "bitter personal screed filled with the grossest misrepresentations, with manifest prevarications, and with lame attempts at the suppression of facts." Whitney was little better than a "legal imbecile." The solicitor general and other "legal pygmies" gave aid and comfort to "the man of crime." Parker also accused the Supreme Court with "knifing the trial judge in the back and allowing the criminal to go free."

After these vitriolic mutual attacks, Parker and the Justice Department attorneys exchanged their criticisms in private correspondence. The tone was less nasty, but the disagreements remained fundamental. Attorney General Harmon credited the judge with "ability and devotion," but chastised him for his recent behavior, which made him appear "disposed to be insubordinate." He suggested that Parker give shorter and less "misleading and declaratory" instructions to juries, thereby avoiding the potential for reversible error. He closed by expressing his strong disapproval of Parker's airing of differences with the Justice Department and Supreme Court in the newspapers.

Parker was unrepentant. In a letter of April 2, 1896 to the attorney general, he denied being insubordinate and accused the Supreme Court of holding an incorrect view of self-defense. He defended his interpretations of other points of law and accused the Justice Department of prejudice against him based on "slander and falsehood." He believed that Attorney General Harmon was charging him with "duplicity and dishonesty." The Justice Department attorneys, Parker said, were too inexperienced in criminal law to pass judgment on his rulings.

For the time being, Parker stopped attacking the Supreme Court and the Justice Department in the newspapers, but he was not content to confine his views to private correspondence. He began to include criticisms of the Court in his courtroom charges to grand and petit juries. He reached a national audience in the June 1896 issue of the *North American Review* in an article entitled "How to Arrest the Increase of Homicides in America." Although the language was more restrained than that of his newspaper salvos, his arguments remained the same, and the Supreme Court was still the main target of his displeasure.

The great problem facing America, wrote Parker, was whether "the man who destroys human life shall be the despotic ruler, or whether the law of the land shall exert its peaceful sway, and by its protecting power secure all men in their lives . . . wherever they may be." He presented alarming statistics: in the past six years there had been 43,902 homicides in the United States, an average of 7,317 per year. The homicide rate had increased dramatically from 1890, when there were 4,290 killings, to 1895, when there were 10,500 killings. In the same six-year period there were 723 legal executions and 1,118 lynchings. The lynchings were being committed "by masses of men who are endeavoring by bloody and improper means to seek a remedy—I mean those who band together as mobs to seek that protection which they fail to obtain under the forms of law."

In the article, Parker quoted Judge Elliot Anthony, president of the Illinois State Bar Association, who believed the problem was the result of a judiciary largely ignorant of criminal law and too concerned with the rights of defendants. Anthony castigated "the great effort . . . to involve every investigation of crime in a network of subtleties, artificial distinctions, and downright quibbles." Parker also quoted from an address by eminent legal authority David Dudley Field to the American Bar Association in 1889 lamenting that "there is no other country calling itself civilized," as far as Field was aware, "where it is so difficult to convict and punish a criminal." Field accused the Supreme Court of "establish[ing] an arbitrary system of rules and regulations" that thwarted efforts to punish criminals.

Parker agreed with these assessments and charged that the terrible state of affairs was caused by: "a morbid, diseased public sentiment, which begets undue sympathy for the criminal, and has none whatever for his murdered victim"; "indifference of the people to the enforcement of the criminal law"; "corrupt verdicts begotten by frauds and perjuries"; "undue exercise of influence, either monetary, social, or otherwise, so that juries are carried away from the line of duty"; and "the indifference and negligence of trial courts." Warming to his subject, Parker leveled his guns at what he believed was the main culprit behind the growing crime rate: the appellate courts. They "exist in order to consider and act on alleged flaws in the records of the trial tribunals" and "make most strenuous efforts, as a rule, to see not when they can affirm but when they can reverse a case." Such conduct "encourages the legal practice that is altogether in the interest of the man of crime."

Parker did not believe the jury system was responsible for the rise in crime. The right to trial by jury, he argued, was "the very bulwark of liberty in this land. . . . It is the source of our greatest peace and the foundation of our hopes for the future." Juries, however, needed to be "guided by courts honest and brave enough to stand by the law and its enforcement." He quoted approvingly the words of Justice Brewer, who said that juries were more trustworthy than appellate courts in securing true justice.

Parker ended his article with suggestions for halting the scourge of rampant crime. First, there must be an effort by the nation's press, statesmen, clergy, and political parties to arouse public sentiment "in favor of vigorous enforcement of the law, the suppression of crime, and the extinction of the [lynch] mob—this disgrace of our Christianity and our civilization." Next, he wanted to "remodel" the state and national appellate court systems, which were "the greatest of all promoters of crime." He called for the creation of courts of criminal appeals "made up of judges learned in the criminal law, and governed by a desire for its speedy and vigorous enforcement." Full records of the trial should be sent to these tribunals, which "should be compelled to pass upon the case as soon as possible" and should base their decision on the merits of the case, not technicalities "concocted by cunning minds." "The guilt or innocence of the party should be the guide." Parker showed some consideration for the accused by agreeing that they should have the right of appeal and that the process should be easy. He proposed that the government pay for counsel if a defendant was unable to do so. Finally, Parker assured his readers that the adoption of his recommendations would increase public confidence in the legal system and abate crime.

National law journals such as the *American Law Review* and the *Chicago Legal News* agreed with Parker's views. They, too, accused the Supreme Court of being more concerned with technicalities than with substance in its review of criminal cases. Like Parker, they attributed the rise in the number of lynchings to the failure of courts, both trial and appellate, to punish murderers.

By the time his article appeared in June 1896, Parker was dying. He was suffering from Bright's disease and complications that were believed to have been caused by overwork. Later in the summer Parker was confined to bed, too weak to carry out his judicial duties. Before then, he had not missed a day of court business because of illness. Circuit Judge Henry C. Caldwell dispatched Oliver P. Shiras, judge of the United State District Court for the Northern District of Iowa, to take over Parker's duties. He did so for only two days, August 27 and 28. The Indian Territory jurisdiction of Parker's court was to terminate on September 1. Accordingly, the court's crier, J. G. Hammersly, on August 28, 1896, intoned, "Oyez! Oyez! The Honorable Circuit and District Courts for the Western District of Arkansas, having criminal jurisdiction of the Indian Territory, are now adjourned, forever."

On the day the court's authority over the Indian Territory ended in 1896, reporter Ada Patterson of the *Saint Louis Republic* appeared in Fort Smith to interview the bedridden judge. Weak and wracked with pain, Parker consented to the interview, no doubt pleased to have one last opportunity to defend his career and condemn his enemies. Patterson found the once sturdy and fit Parker a feeble, paunchy figure whose hair and beard had turned almost completely white, though he was only fifty-seven years old. She was also surprised to find him "the gentlest of men, this alleged sternest of judges." Mary Parker fanned her husband's brow with a palm leaf as he answer the reporter's questions.

Much of what he said in the interview was by then familiar. The justices of the Supreme Court were not versed in criminal law; juries had to be led to render justice; his critics had no notion of the type of hardened criminals his court had to contend with. He expressed sympathy for the families of murder victims and gently criticized the "good ladies" of the community who brought "flowers and jellies" to prisoners sentenced to the gallows. He admonished these well-intentioned women for forgetting the families whose fathers had been taken away from them by the murderers.

Parker had always maintained that it was the certainty, not the severity, of punishment that was the surest deterrent of crime. But readers of the *Republic* must have been surprised at Parker's response to the reporter's inevitable question about capital punishment: "I favor its abolition, provided that there is a certainty of punishment." Throughout his many years on the bench, Parker said, he had "ever had the single aim of justice in view." "Do equal and exact justice" had been his motto. He reiterated the words he had so often spoken to grand juries: "Permit no innocent man to suffer; let no guilty man escape."

In the course of the interview, Parker again praised the Native Americans of the Indian Territory for being "religiously-inclined, law-abiding and authority-respecting." Congress, he said, had deprived "the Indian Country of the moral force of a strong Federal Court." He put his criticism of federal Indian policy even more bluntly in a statement in the September 18, 1896, *Fort Smith Elevator*: "The territory was set apart for the Indians in 1828. The government at that time promised them protection. That promise has been ignored. The only protection that has ever been afforded them is through the courts. To us who have been located on this borderland, has fallen the task of acting as protectors." Patterson concluded her newspaper story by agreeing with people in Fort Smith who had told her, "He is a good man": "I am glad to have the honor of knowing this alleged cruel judge. It is darkly, indeed, the press and people view him through the glass of distance."

Any hope of Parker's recovery was soon abandoned. Circuit Judge Walter Sanborn ordered John E. Carland of the federal court for South Dakota to preside over the November 1896 term of the court for the Western District of Arkansas.

Many friends visited Parker in his last days, and his sons, Charles, an attorney in Saint Louis, and James, a student at the University of Michigan, reached Fort Smith in time to bid their father farewell. Judge Parker slipped into a coma on November 16, but revived and summoned Father Laurence Smyth to baptize him into his wife Mary's faith, Roman Catholicism. After doing so, the priest administered the last rites. Isaac C. Parker's ordeal ended on November 17, 1896, when he died at age fifty-eight.

Epilogue

A Great and Experienced Trial Judge

ISAAC Charles Parker's funeral, Fort Smith's largest up to that time, took place on November 18, 1896. Flags flew at half-mast in honor of the town's best-known citizen. Family, close friends and associates, and members of the fraternal orders to which he had belonged attended the service, held at the Parker home on North 13th Street. Judge F. F. Bryant delivered the eulogy. Parker, said Bryant, "was eminently a man for the time and place, and seemed providentially called to the duty he performed." Bryant told his listeners of Parker's successful effort to clean up the corrupt court that he took over in 1875 and his mighty struggle to stem the tide of lawlessness in the country's "worst jurisdiction."

Thousands of mourners riding in every available conveyance followed the casket to the Fort Smith National Cemetery. Father Smyth conducted the graveside services. Comrades in the Grand Army of the Republic and lodge brothers from the Knights of Honor and Odd Fellows attended, along with court personnel, members of the bar, journalists, and townspeople. At the conclusion of the formal funeral rites, Principal Chief of the Creek Nation Pleasant Porter laid a garland of wildflowers on the casket. Sadie Dove, an Indian woman, placed flowers on the grave. The plain soldier's headstone bears only the name "Isaac C. Parker" and the number "4000." Also buried in the cemetery are District Attorney William H. H. Clayton, United States Marshal Jacob Yoes, and a number of the deputy marshals who had served Parker's court faithfully. Mary Parker, who died in 1926, is buried next to her husband.

News of the judge's death brought cheers from the inmates of the federal jail in Fort Smith ("Is he dead? Whoopee!"). His passing, however, had no effect on the men behind bars there. Their sentences, including executions, continued as ordered.

On September 1, 1896, the day before the people of Indian Territory were to be "emancipated" from the courts at Fort Smith, Arkansas, and Paris, Texas there was public rejoicing. The editor of the newspaper in Purcell, in the Chickasaw Nation, welcomed the end of "judicial bondage": "Our relief from Arkansas and Texas serfdom is too heartily welcome to our people to permit the day of our great deliverance to pass unnoticed." The relief was short-lived; the Curtis Act of 1898 abolished the tribal courts and declared Indian law unenforceable in federal courts. In 1907 Congress admitted the state of Oklahoma, created by combining the Indian and Oklahoma territories.

Only as a court with jurisdiction in the Indian Territory was the federal tribunal at Fort Smith "adjourned, forever" in 1896. The United States District Court for the Western District of Arkansas continues to exist and now embraces about one-half of the state. John H. Rogers, co-author of the legislation that allowed appeals from Fort Smith to the Supreme Court, succeeded Parker as judge for the Western District.

Once the court's docket was cleared of Indian Territory cases, there was no need for the infamous gallows, which were dismantled and burned in 1897. The old barracks-courthouse, the notorious jail below, the adjoining new jail, the commissary building where the judge's chambers were housed, a reconstructed gallows, and the National Cemetery are now all part of the Fort Smith National Historic Site, established in 1961 and administered by the National Park Service. Despite concern over Parker's supposed racism, Congress authorized the construction of the Isaac C. Parker Federal Building in Fort Smith in 1995, and it opened the following year. Otherwise, there are few physical reminders of his extraordinary presence in the community. A tornado wrecked the Parker home in 1898, and the site was occupied by Fort Smith's new Carnegie Library in 1907.

The 1898 twister also destroyed Parker's personal papers, and few examples of his private correspondence exist in research libraries, leaving biographers with only a limited knowledge of his personal life. Much more is known of the public man, but assessing his career is not easy. Perhaps historian Jeffrey Burton summed it up best: "On the whole, Parker was a much better servant than a bad system deserved; but when that system was improved, he rebelled against it."

Opinions about Parker among the people of the Indian Territory were divided. Many resented the authority his and other outside federal courts exercised. Others had the same view the judge had of himself: as a friend and protector of the Indians. By and large, the people of the territory respected and trusted him. They may not have regretted the end of his court's power over them, but when he died, many paid tribute to the judge who had figured so prominently in their lives. As one of their spokesmen put it: "The Indian people . . . have lost one of their staunchest friends and one of the ablest and most consistent defenders of their rights under the treaties with the United States. The good people of the Territory knew him to be an upright judge, a lawyer of towering ability, a citizen of the very highest standards, a gentleman of the most refined character, a friend of unswerving fidelity and an example to society."

Parker sincerely believed that he had worked for the best interests of the Native Americans within his Indian Territory jurisdiction. In addition to his fight against violent crime, he sought to punish whites who illegally invaded the region as would-be settlers, and he strove to protect the Indians from whiskey dealers and timber poachers. Yet, in several of his rulings, Parker placed limits on self-government in the Indian nations and helped to pave the way for the eventual white domination of the territory. He occasionally deferred to the tribal courts when there was a question of jurisdiction, but more often he ruled that cases belonged in his court. In conflicts between federal authority and Indian claims of sovereignty, he regularly denied that the Indian Nations had sovereign power. Federal power—especially as wielded by his court—was supreme.

Parker was quick to claim jurisdiction for his own court and reluctant to yield it to others, whether tribal, state, or federal. In criminal and civil cases involving jurisdictional conflicts, he consistently ruled that they belonged before him. Such cases became particularly conspicuous when Congress began whittling down his Indian Territory jurisdiction; he continued to insist that the Fort Smith court retained its authority in areas manifestly beyond his judicial reach. In several habeas corpus proceedings, he appears to have been sensitive to the civil liberties of the accused, but he was in fact more concerned with protecting and extending the authority of his court and denying jurisdiction to other tribunals.

Parker's unyielding conviction that his judicial power was indispensable in the struggle against lawlessness in the Indian Territory was, more than anything else, what inclined him to fight for his court's prerogatives. He had come to equate the continued authority of his court with the well-being of the people of the Indian Territory, and he believed that other courts there, both tribal and federal, were not the bulwarks against crime that his was. Not only did he see his court as the most effective instrument for combating crime in the territory, he was apparently convinced that he was the only judge dedicated enough to be entrusted with the responsibility of bringing law and order to the troubled area.

Parker's determination to guard against the encroachments of other courts was most apparent in his battles with the Supreme Court. His embarrassingly public quarrels with the Court also brought him into conflict with the Justice Department. Until 1889 there had been no appeal of capital cases from the Western District of Arkansas. Afterward, the Supreme Court reversed the majority of cases, including noncapital cases, coming to it from Fort Smith. Parker and his supporters maintained that the members of the Court were unversed in criminal law and ignorant of the vicious character of the criminals hauled before him. He was also convinced that the reversals were based on trifling legal technicalities. In some cases, this conclusion was true. In most, however, the grounds for reversal were serious and substantial: prejudicing juries against the defendant and in favor of the prosecution; clinging to interpretations of the common law that other judges had rejected (for example, the duty to retreat); and refusing to be guided by the rulings of the Supreme Court and the admonitions of the Justice Department. His stubborn and intemperate resistance to the authority of the Court is explained largely by the many years in which there was no appeal from his sentences. Accustomed to having things his own way, he bitterly resented what he saw as unwarranted interference in matters about which he knew best.

Judged by the standards of a later day, and even by the changing standards of his own time, Parker's brand of justice appears unduly harsh. Yet he has always had his defenders. No less an authority than John H. Wigmore, author of the standard treatise on evidence, has written that the Supreme Court was wrong in its "attempts to assume the position of monitor over a great and experienced trial judge." Associate Justice and later Chief Justice William H. Rehnquist has approvingly referred to Parker in opinions in capital punishment cases written almost a century after the Hanging Judge's death.

Balanced against Parker's reputation as a stern dispenser of draconian justice are several facts that show him to be much less rigid and severe than commonly supposed. Unlike Chief Justice Rehnquist, he was not an ardent supporter of the death penalty. Parker believed the certainty of punishment was more important than the severity of punishment as a deterrent to crime. As biographer Roger H. Tuller has pointed out, one of Parker's objections to the Supreme Court reversals was that the resultant delays and retrials undermined the element of certainty of punishment.

Parker, influenced by his religious convictions, believed that even the most hardened malefactors were capable of redemption, either in this world or the next. He attributed lawbreaking not to an inherently evil nature but rather to a bad environment and the lack of moral guidance early in life. It was his policy to send long-term prisoners to penal institutions that offered the best opportunities for reform. Compassion and a sense of fairness are evident in the many instances in which he urged executive clemency because of reservations about the guilt of those convicted, mitigating circumstances, or his belief that the punishment was excessive.

Parker saved most of his compassion for the victims of crime, particularly those left fatherless. Similarly, in civil cases, he voiced strong disapproval of the law's failure to take into account the suffering of the families of those whose lives had been taken by the apparent negligence of railroads. Among federal judges, he stood out as a friend to people who sought damages for deaths and injuries from train accidents. It is reasonable to believe that in these cases, he steered juries to the conclusions he desired, just as he did in criminal cases.

Isaac C. Parker deserves to be thought of as something other than a fanatical hanging judge who ended his days in bitter and futile conflict with the nation's highest court. It is far better that he be remembered as a conscientious and hard-working jurist dedicated to imposing the rule of law on a notoriously violent land.

Appendix A

Isaac C. Parker and Popular Culture

JUDGE Isaac C. Parker has appeared as a character in several novels, motion pictures, and other forms of popular culture. None claims to be historically accurate, and in some cases they display considerable creative license, but most make for good reading or viewing. Several of the literary and screen representations of Parker and his Fort Smith court are surprisingly on the mark. As a general rule, the films and novels that pay attention to historical fact are superior in most respects to those that do not. The best fictional representations of Parker sometimes capture the essence of the man and his times better than the most reputable historical scholarship. When an author or filmmaker has not gone beyond the myth of the Hanging Judge, the result is usually inferior.

Perhaps the best-known work of fiction in which Parker appears is Charles Portis's marvelous novel *True Grit* (1968). In a courtroom scene, Portis depicts Judge Parker presiding evenhandedly over a murder trial wherein the novel's protagonist, Deputy Marshal Rooster Cogburn, provides blunt and salty testimony. Later in the book, Cogburn speaks approvingly of Parker, even though he calls him an "old carpetbagger." There is also a gallows scene in which George Maledon hangs three men; mention of prisoners being sent to the Detroit House of Correction; and references to the old jail, Henry Starr, and the Dalton brothers. The film version of *True Grit* (1969), starring John Wayne, has veteran character actor James Westerfield playing Judge Parker. In a sequel, *Rooster Cogburn* (1975), John McIntire portrays a kindly, soft-spoken, more fleshed-out Parker. Nevertheless, the earlier film does a better job of showing how the Parker court functioned.

In the excellent film *Hang 'em High* (1968), Clint Eastwood plays a deputy marshal employed by the court of "Judge Fenton," a character obviously modeled after Parker. Fenton, well played by Pat Hingle, is a dedicated, conscientious jurist. Although he feels duty-bound to witness executions from the window of his chambers, he finds that watching the hangings is a painful experience. Later in the film, he cries out, in language that Parker himself might have employed, against the awful moral responsibility his job imposes.

There are a number of Parker portrayals in films of lesser quality that depart significantly from historical reality; for example, *The Last Ride of the Dalton Gang*, a 1979 film made for television, with Dale Robertson in the role of Parker. Even though he is made-up to look more like the Fort Smith judge than other actors who have played the role, his portrayal is based on the common misconception of Parker as a law-enforcing zealot. Upon learning that Deputy Marshal Bob Dalton and his brothers have linked up with the Bill Doolin gang and have engaged in horse theft, Parker rides into "Oklahoma Territory" and tells the Daltons and their cohorts that if they do not leave the territory immediately, he will hang them—presumably without a trial.

In a 1919 six-reel, silent motion picture, *A Debtor to the Law*, real-life outlaw Henry Starr plays himself. Much of the film deals with his robbery of a bank in Stroud, Oklahoma. Richard Slotkin's 1988 novel, *The Return of Henry Starr*, is a fictional account of the making of *A Debtor to the Law*. Parker does not appear as a full-fledged character in the novel, but there are references to George Maledon and to Henry Starr's "Aunt Belle." Like the real Henry Starr, the fictional Starr has no love for the man who twice sentenced him to death. He sees him as an "old bastard" who "likes his hangings." The protagonist finds amused satisfaction in having Parker played by the director of the film, who has a thick eastern European accent; in a silent film, the accent of course makes no difference to an audience.

Two novels by Douglas C. Jones include excellent fictional representations of Parker and his court. In *Winding Stair* (1979), Deputy Marshal Oscar Schiller tracks down a band of killers and rapists that bears more than a passing resemblance to the Rufus Buck gang; one of its members seems to be based on the real-life murderer Johnny Pointer. *The Search for Temperance Moon* (1991) also features Schiller, who unravels the mystery of the title character's death. Temperance Moon is based on Belle Starr, and Jewel Moon, madam of a Fort Smith brothel, is based on Belle's daughter, Pearl. Several other characters of both novels are recognizable representations of actual persons associated with Parker. In *The Search for Temperance Moon*, the judge presides over the climactic murder trial with skill and impartiality. Although Schiller is an exceptionally able and courageous officer, he uses cocaine and, like some of the flesh-and-blood deputies of the Fort Smith court, pads his expense account.

Well-versed in Parker and his milieu, author Jones offers several astute observations on both. For example, he writes of "a certain element" in the gallery at any Parker trial, particularly reporters from Kansas City, Saint Louis, and Little Rock, "who came expecting a circus atmosphere." They were "usually disappointed and astonished to find that this court, so well publicized as the home of the 'Hanging Judge,' looked exactly like any other federal court and operated exactly like any other federal court." Among the many indications that Jones knows more about the Parker court than authors of works purporting to be "authentic," he notes in *Winding Stair* that when Parker assumed his judicial duties at Fort Smith, "capital crimes and their punishment were proscribed by law, a fact seldom remarked upon in print or on the floor of Congress. In pronouncing death sentences, Parker often explained to the condemned that the letter of the law, which he was bound to observe, left him no alternative." The novel's protagonist, Assistant Prosecutor Eben Pay, describes the judge as "a gentle and genial man."

In the author's introduction to *Hanging Judge* (1969), novelist Elmer Kelton writes: "Judge Isaac C. Parker is sometimes portrayed as a ruthless and fanatical hangman, which is an injustice to a well-meaning, dedicated man." From this, readers can correctly assume that Kelton has a good knowledge of the judge and his times. The fast-moving story, however, is less about Parker than about a group of his deputy marshals who are pitted against a band of murderous whiskey runners. The main character is Justin Moffitt, who is just beginning his career as a deputy. His mentor is tough, resourceful, and honorable Sam Dark. Assisting them is black deputy George Grider, an expert tracker. Rice Pegler is a bigoted and cruel deputy in league with the whiskey runners. Parker is characterized as a jurist sincerely devoted to the rule of law, whose sense of justice at times works against the deputies and to the benefit of the lawbreakers. Real-life marshal Jacob Yoes also appears in the novel.

Larry McMurtry and Diana Ossana are more interested in telling a good story than in capturing historical reality in their novel *Zeke and Ned* (1997). By turns wryly humorous and violent, it is loosely based on real-life Indian Territory desperados Zeke Proctor and Ned Christie. Isaac Parker is depicted as dignified and gruff, but admirable.

The most bizarre portrayal of Judge Parker is in Daniel Freeman's two-act play *Jesse and the Bandit Queen* (1976), an enjoyable mixture of fact, fantasy, and myth. There are only two characters, Jesse James and Belle Starr, but throughout the play, they take on the roles of other persons who figure in their lives. At one point, Belle tells the audience that "I had my share of trials. . . . And they loved me. I dressed up real good and my trials was more famous than God. I met the Judge. Judge Parker, The Hanging Judge, and I made him mine." Jesse then assumes the persona of Parker, who is trying Belle for horse theft. He announces that "I am the law.

The only law. Parker's law west of the Pecos. I have gallows for twelve. A Parker's dozen. Would you care to try one?" He threatens Belle with hanging, even though he had "never had a woman before me. No woman has ever hanged west of the Pecos." Belle saves herself from this fate by seducing the judge. Elsewhere in the play are mentions of Blue Duck (whom Belle calls "my own sweet Cherokee"), George Maledon, Jack Spaniard, various members of the Starr family, and Belle's imprisonment in Detroit.

Most of the above literary and film treatments of Parker are sympathetic and respectful. Given Parker's fearful reputation, this tendency is surprising. Writers such as Portis, Jones, and Kelton learned enough about the man to show him as something other than a single-minded fanatic. In another novel, Ray Hogan's *The Doomsday Marshal and the Hanging Judge* (1987), the judge is a sadist who goes throughout the West apparently with a roving commission to hang people. He bears no resemblance to Parker and is probably not intended to.

In another work, a ballad entitled "A Prisoner for Life," the singer laments his bleak future behind bars. The song has been attributed to William Alexander, who had been convicted of murder in Parker's court in 1890. The Supreme Court reversed the conviction and Alexander was released after two trials. Since he did not face the likelihood of life imprisonment, there is doubt as to his authorship of the ballad, and some authorities believe that it is of Irish origin.

The variety of manifestations of Parker's image reflect the different perceptions of him and attest to his hold on the public's imagination. Whether shown as a draconian dispenser of vengeful justice or as a properly professional jurist, Isaac C. Parker remains an enduring presence in American popular culture.

Appendix B

Court Cases

The Federal Cases, Comprising Cases Argued and Determined in the Circuit and District Courts of the United States. 300 vols. St. Paul, MN: West Publishing Co., 1880–1925:

Connor v. *Scott,* 6 Fed. Cases 313 (1876)
Culver et al. v. *County of Crawford,* 6 Fed. Cases 948 (1877)
Culver et al. v. *Woodruff County,* 6 Fed. Cases 949 (1878)
Ex parte Kenyon, 14 Fed. Cases 353 (1878)
National Bank of Western Arkansas v. *Sebastian County,* 17 Fed. Cases 1209 (1879)
Ex parte Reynolds, 20 Fed. Cases 582 (1879)
United States v. *Reese,* 27 Fed. Cases 742 (1879)

The Federal Reporter. Cases Argued and Determined in the Circuit and District Courts of the United States. 31 vols. St. Paul, MN: West Publishing Co., 1894–98:

Bland and others v. *Fleeman and others,* 29 Fed. 669 (1887)
Briscoe v. *Southern Kan. Ry. Co.,* 40 Fed. 273 (1889)
Brooks et al. v. *Fry et al.,* 45 Fed. 776 (1891)
Ex parte Brown, 40 Fed. 71 (1889)
Ex parte Brown, 40 Fed. 81 (1889)
Cherokee Nation v. *Southern Kan. R. Co.,* 33 Fed. 900 (1888)
Crawson v. *Western Union Tel. Co.,* 47 Fed. 544 (1891)
Daniels v. *Benedict et al.,* 50 Fed. 347 (1892)
Dryfus v. *Burnes et ux.,* 53 Fed. 410 (1892)
Dwyer et al. v. *St. Louis & S. F. R. Co.,* 52 Fed. 87 (1892)
Ex parte Farley, 40 Fed. 66 (1889)

Foltz et al. v. *St. Louis & S. F. Ry. Co.*, 60 Fed. 316 (1894)
Gowen v. *Harley*, 56 Fed. 973 (1893)
Hoover v. *Crawford County*, 39 Fed. 7 (1889)
James v. *St. Louis & S. F. Ry. Co.*, 46 Fed. 47 (1891)
Kansas & A. Val. Ry. Co. v. *Le Flore*, 49 Fed. 119 (1892)
Kansas & A. Val. Ry. Co. v. *Payne et al.*, 49 Fed. 114 (1892)
Ex parte Kyle, 67 Fed. 306 (1895)
Liggett & Myer Tobacco Co. v. *Hynes*, 20 Fed. 883 (1884)
Lincoln National Bank of Lincoln, Ill. v. *Perry et al.*, 66 Fed. 887 (1895)
In re Marquandt, 46 Fed. 52 (1891)
Ex parte McClusky, 40 Fed. 71 (1889)
In re Monroe, 46 Fed. 52 (1891)
Ex parte Morgan, 20 Fed. 298 (1883)
Payne et al. v. *Kansas & A. Val. R. Co.*, 46 Fed. 546 (1891)
St. Louis & S. F. Ry. Co. et al. v. *Bennett*, 69 Fed. 525 (1895)
St. Louis & S. F. Ry. Co. et al. v. *Bennett*, 69 Fed. 530 (1895)
St. Louis & S. F. R. Co. v. *Foltz*, 52 Fed. 627 (1892)
St. Louis & S. F. Ry. Co. et al. v. *Hicks*, 69 Fed. 584 (1895)
St. Louis & S. F. Ry. Co. et al. v. *Hicks* (two cases), 69 Fed. 531 (1895)
St. Louis & S. F. Ry. Co. et al. v. *Hicks* (two cases), 79 Fed. 262 (1897)
St. Louis & S. F. Ry. Co. v. *James*, 73 Fed. 1022 (1896)
St. Louis & S. F. Ry. Co. et al. v. *Miles*, 69 Fed. 530 (1895)
St. Louis & S. F. Ry. Co. v. *Miles*, 79 Fed. 257 (1897)
St. Louis & S. F. Ry. Co. v. *Whittle et al.*, 74 Fed. 296 (1896)
S[c]humacher v. *St. Louis & S. F. R. Co.*, 39 Fed. 174 (1889)
Stephens v. *St. Louis & S. F. R. Co.*, 47 Fed. 530 (1891)
Thompson v. *McReynolds and others*, 29 Fed. 657 (1887)
Tilley et ux. v. *American Bldg. & Loan Ass'n.*, 52 Fed. 618 (1892)
United States v. *Boyd et al.*, 45 Fed. 851 (1890)
United States v. *Culver et al.*, 52 Fed. 81 (1892)
United States v. *Ellis*, 51 Fed. 808 (1892)
United States v. *Howell et al.*, 56 Fed. 21 (1892)

United States v. *Hudson*, 65 Fed. 68 (1894)
United States ex rel. McIntosh et al. v. *Crawford et al.*, 47 Fed. 561 (1891)
United States v. *Payne*, 8 Fed. 883 (1881)
United States v. *Rogers*, 23 Fed. 658 (1885)
United States v. *Soule and others*, 30 Fed. 918 (1887)
Western Coal & Mining Co. v. *Ingraham*, 70 Fed. 219 (1895)
Ex parte Wilson, 40 Fed. 66 (1889)
In re Wolf[e], 27 Fed. 606 (1886)

United States Reports:

Acers v. *United States*, 164 U.S. 388 (1896)
Alberty v. *United States*, 162 U.S. 499 (1896)
Alexander v. *United States*, 138 U.S. 353 (1891)
Allen v. *United States*, 150 U.S. 551 (1893)
Allen v. *United States*, 157 U.S. 675 (1895)
Allen v. *United States*, 164 U.S. 492 (1896)
Allison v. *United States*, 160 U.S. 203 (1895)
Babe Beard v. *United States*, 158 U.S. 550 (1895)
Boyd v. *United States*, 142 U.S. 450 (1892)
Brown v. *United States*, 150 U.S. 93 (1893)
Brown v. *United States*, 159 U.S. 100 (1895)
Brown v. *United States*, 164 U.S. 221 (1896)
Brown v. *United States*, 256 U.S. 335 (1921)
Buck and others v. *United States*, 163 U.S. 678 (1896)
Carver v. *United States*, 160 U.S. 553 (1896)
Carver v. *United States*, 164 U.S. 694 (1897)
Cherokee Nation v. *Southern Kansas Ry. Co.*, 135 U.S. 641 (1890)
Coleman v. *Balkhorn*, 451 U.S. 949 (1891)
Collins v. *United States*, 150 U.S. 62 (1893)
Crain v. *United States*, 162 U.S. 625 (1896)
Crumpton v. *United States*, 138 U.S. 361 (1891)
Davis v. *United States*, 160 U.S. 469 (1895)
Davis v. *United States*, 165 U.S. 373 (1897)

Dyer v. *United States*, 164 U.S. 704 (1896)

Goldsby alias *Cherokee Bill* v. *United States*, 160 U.S. 70 (1895)

Goldsby alias *Cherokee Bill* v. *United States*, 163 U.S. 688 (1896)

Gourko v. *United States*, 153 U.S. 183 (1894)

Graves v. *United States*, 150 U.S. 118 (1893)

Hall v. *United States*, 150 U.S. 76 (1893)

Hickory v. *United States*, 151 U.S. 303 (1894)

Hickory v. *United States*, 160 U.S. 408 (1896)

Hicks v. *United States*, 150 U.S. 442 (1893)

Holder v. *United States*, 150 U.S. 91 (1893)

Howell et al. v. *United States*, 163 U.S. 690 (1896)

Hudson v. *Parker*, 156 U.S. 277 (1895)

Isaacs v. *United States*, 159 U.S. 487 (1895)

Johnson alias *Overton* v. *United States*, 157 U.S. 320 (1895)

Kettenring v. *United States*, 168 U.S. 703 (1897)

King v. *United States*, 164 U.S. 701 (1896)

Lewis v. *United States*, 146 U.S. 370 (1892)

Lowenfield v. *Phelps et al.*, 484 U.S. 231 (1898)

Lucas v. *United States*, 163 U.S. 612 (1896)

Luckey v. *United States*, 163 U.S. 692 (1896)

Ex parte Mayfield, 141 U.S. 107 (1891)

McElroy et al. v. *United States*, 164 U.S. 76 (1896)

Mills v. *United States*, 164 U.S. 644 (1897)

Nofire et al. v. *United States*, 164 U.S. 657 (1897)

Oliphant v. *Suquamish Indian Tribe et al.*, 435 U.S. 191 (1978)

Pierce et al. v. *United States*, 160 U.S. 355 (1896)

Pointer v. *United States*, 151 U.S. 396 (1894)

Rowe v. *United States*, 164 U.S. 546 (1896)

St. Louis & San Francisco Ry. Co. v. *James*, 161 U.S. 545 (1896)

St. Louis & San Francisco Ry. Co. v. *McBride*, 141 U.S. 127 (1891)

St. Louis & San Francisco Ry. Co. v. *Schumacher*, 152 U.S. 77 (1894)

Sarlls v. *United States,* 152 U.S. 570 (1894)
Famous Smith v. *United States,* 151 U.S. 50 (1894)
Smith v. *United States,* 161 U.S. 85 (1896)
Southern Kansas Ry. Co. v. *Briscoe,* 144 U.S. 133 (1892)
Starr v. *United States,* 153 U.S. 614 (1894)
Starr v. *United States,* 164 U.S. 627 (1897)
Talton v. *Mayes,* 163 U.S. 376 (1896)
Thompson v. *United States,* 155 U.S. 271 (1894)
Thornton v. *United States,* 163 U.S. 707 (1896)
Tucker v. *United States,* 151 U.S. 164 (1894)
United States v. *Perryman,* 100 U.S. 235 (1880)
Wilkey alias *Davis* v. *United States,* 163 U.S. 712 (1896)
Wilson v. *United States,* 162 U.S. 613 (1896)

Reports of Cases at Law and in Equity Argued and Determined in the Supreme Court of the State of Arkansas:

Elmore v. *State,* 45 Ark. 243 (1885)

Bibliographical Essay

THE principal archival sources for Isaac C. Parker and his court are the Records of the United States District Court for the Western District of Arkansas, RG 21, National Archives, Southwest Region, Fort Worth, Texas. Case files, transcripts of records, and briefs of civil cases brought to the United States Circuit Court of Appeals for the Eighth Circuit are in RG 276, National Archives, Central Plains Region, Kansas City, Missouri. Parker's record of militia service is in the Missouri State Archives.

Among congressional publications that give details on the Fort Smith court, its personnel, and its jail are several House and Senate Reports, Journals, Miscellaneous Documents, and Executive Documents. Parker's record as a member of the United States House of Representatives is in the *Congressional Record* for the 42d and 43d Congresses. The legislative history of changes that affected the Court for the Western District of Arkansas is in the *Congressional Record* for the 42d, 48th, 50th, 51st, and 54th Congresses. Relevant legislation is in the *Statutes at Large of the United States of America*, volumes 9, 10, 16, 18, 19, and 23-29. The *Ninth, Tenth,* and *Eleventh Census of the United States* (1870, 1880, and 1890) have population figures and economic data for Missouri, Arkansas, and the Indian Territory. The *Annual Reports of the Attorney-General,* 1875–96, contain material on the relationship between Department of Justice officials and the Parker court, including recommendations for executive clemency. Cases appealed to the Supreme Court from the verdicts and rulings of Parker's court are in *The United States*

Reports. Cases Adjudged in the Supreme Court (see Court Cases). Two quasi-official series contain Parker's published opinions and jury charges: *The Federal Cases, Comprising Cases Argued and Determined in the Circuit and District Courts of the United States*, 31 vols. (St. Paul, MN: West Publishing Co., 1880–1925); and *The Federal Reporter. Cases Argued and Determined in the Circuit Courts and District Courts of the United States*, vols. 8-79 (St. Paul, MN: West Publishing Co., 1881–97). The *Federal Reporter* also includes cases decided by the Circuit Court of Appeals for the Eighth Circuit. For lists of Parker cases found in both publications, see Court Cases.

State government publications that pertain to aspects of Parker's career are *Wagner's Missouri Statutes, 1869, General Statutes of Missouri, 1864–1870*, and *Reports of Cases at Law and in Equity Argued and Determined in the Supreme Court of the State of Arkansas.*

The first book to treat Isaac C. Parker and his court appeared soon after the judge's death—*Hell on the Border: He Hanged Eighty-Eight Men* by S. W. Harman (1898; reprint, Lincoln: University of Nebraska Press, 1992). Harman, who served on juries of the District Court for the Western District of Arkansas, provides information not found elsewhere. Unfortunately, many of Harman's anecdotes are of doubtful authenticity, and much of the volume is devoted to extolling the courtroom triumphs of attorney J. Warren Reed, based on information Reed himself apparently supplied.

Hanging Judge by historian Fred Harvey Harrington (1951; reprint, Norman: University of Oklahoma Press, 1996) stood for many years as the best biography and the first scholarly work on Parker. Larry D. Ball wrote useful introductions to both the Harman and Harrington reprint editions. A few popular accounts of Parker's life exist but add little of value; for example, Homer Croy, *He Hanged Them High: An Authentic Account of the Fanatical Judge Who Hanged Eighty-Eight Men* (New York: Duell, Sloan and Pearce, 1952); and J. Gladstone Emery, *Court of the*

Damned: Being a Factual Account of the Court of Isaac C. Parker and the Life and Times of the Indian Territory and Old Fort Smith (New York: Comet Press Books, 1959).

A welcome addition to the literature about Parker is Roger H. Tuller, *"Let No Guilty Man Escape": A Judicial Biography of "Hanging Judge" Isaac C. Parker* (Norman: University of Oklahoma Press, 2001). Likely to remain the standard biography for many years, it is well-researched, clearly written, and insightful.

Two unpublished theses cover Parker's career: James Murphy, "The Work of Judge Parker in the United States District Court for the Western District of Arkansas" (M.A. thesis, University of Oklahoma, 1939); and Mary Margaret Stolberg, "Politician, Populist, Reformer: A Reexamination of 'Hanging Judge' Isaac Parker" M.A. thesis, University of Virginia, 1986). The latter is particularly good on Parker's relations with the Department of Justice. Two subsequent articles by Mary M. Stolberg also add much to our understanding of the man: "Politician, Populist, Reformer: A Reexamination of 'Hanging Judge' Isaac C. Parker," *Arkansas Historical Quarterly* 47 (Spring 1988): 3-28, and "The Evolution of Frontier Justice: The Case of Isaac C. Parker," *Prologue* 20 (Spring 1988):7-23.

Of several brief treatments of Parker's life, the most valuable is Larry D. Ball's entry in *American National Biography* (New York: Oxford University Press, 1999). Others include the Parker obituary in *American Law Review* 31 (January-February 1897): 115–17; Harry P. Daily, "Judge Isaac C. Parker," *Chronicles of Oklahoma* 11 (March 1933): 673–90; Guy Nichols, Leo Allison, and Thomas Crowson, "Judge Isaac Parker: Myths and Legends Aside," Pamphlet No. 1, prepared by the U.S. Park Service (Fort Smith National Historic Site, n.d.); Joel D. Treese, ed., *Biographical Directory of the American Congress, 1774-1996* (Alexandria VA: CQ Directories, 1997); and Wanda Ross, "Memories of Fort Smith's Feared 'Hanging Judge,'" *The Ozark Mountaineer* 44 (October-November 1996). The Fort Smith

National Historic Site has an excellent Web site on Parker, prepared by Eric Leonard: http://nps.gov/fosm/history/judgeparker.

Glenn Shirley, *Law West of Fort Smith: A History of Frontier Justice in Indian Territory, 1834-1896* (Lincoln: University of Nebraska Press, 1968), though not a biography, is indispensable for any study of Parker and his times. It includes a "Chronology of Hangings," two typical jury charges, and lists of commutations, pardons, reversals, and acquittals. Other works that deal with the problems of law enforcement in the Indian Territory include Wayne Gard, *Frontier Justice* (Norman: University of Oklahoma Press, 1949); William T. Hagan, *Indian Police and Judges: Experiments in Acculturation and Control* (New Haven: Yale University Press, 1966); Michael L. Tate, *The Frontier Army in the Settlement of the West* (Norman: University of Oklahoma Press, 1999); and William A. Dobak, "Fort Riley's Black Soldiers and the Army's Changing Role in the West," *Kansas History: A Journal of the Central Plains* 22 (Autumn 1999): 215–27. A good overview of law enforcement in the Indian Territory before, during, and after Parker's time is Bobby L. Blackburn, "Oklahoma Law Enforcement Since 1803" (Ph.D. diss., University of Oklahoma, 1979). A full study of a recurring infraction of the law is Bradley W. Kidder, "Who Took the Trees? A Review of Timber Trespass Litigation in the Federal Court for the Western District of Arkansas Under the Administration of Judge Isaac C. Parker, 1875-1896" (M.A. thesis, University of Arkansas, 1996).

The activities of the marshals and deputy marshals of Parker's court are put into national perspective in Frederick S. Calhoun, *The Lawmen: United States Marshals and Their Deputies, 1789-1989* (Washington: Smithsonian Institution Press, 1989). Works specifically concerned with the marshals and deputy marshals at Fort Smith include C. H. McKennon, *Iron Men: A Saga of the Deputy United States Marshals Who Rode the Indian Territory* (Garden City, NY: Doubleday & Co., 1967); Daniel Littlefield, "Negro Marshals in the Indian

Territory," *Journal of Negro History* 56 (April 1971): 77–87; Charles J. Rector, "D. P. Upham, Woodruff County Carpetbagger," *Arkansas Historical Quarterly* 59 (Spring 2000): 59–75; and Nudie E. Williams, "United States vs. Bass Reeves: Black Lawman on Trial," *Chronicles of Oklahoma* 68 (Summer 1990): 154–67. Paul Trachtman, *The Gunfighters* (Alexandria, VA: Time-Life Books, 1974) contains the printed rules and regulations issued to the deputies.

Information about the federal court system of which Parker's tribunal was a part can be found in Theodore J. Fetter, *A History of the United States Court of Appeals for the Eighth Circuit* (n.p.: Judicial Conference of the United States Bicentennial Committee, 1977); Stephen B. Presser, *Studies in the History of the United States Courts of the Third Circuit* (Washington: Government Publications Office, 1982); Edwin C. Surrency, *History of the Federal Courts* (New York: Oceana Publications, 1987); and Larry D. Ball, "Before the Hanging Judge: The Origins of the United States District Court for the Western District of Arkansas," *Arkansas Historical Quarterly* 49 (Autumn 1990): 199–213.

Several facets of the legal history of Parker's time are discussed in Grant Gilmore, *The Ages of American Law* (New Haven: Yale University Press, 1977); Kermit L. Hall, *The Magic Mirror: Law in American History* (New York: Oxford University Press, 1989); and Samuel Walker, *Popular Justice: A History of American Criminal Justice* (New York: Oxford University Press, 1998).

Parker's difficulties with the United States Supreme Court are treated in Michael J. Brodhead, *David J. Brewer: The Life of a Supreme Court Justice, 1837-1910* (Carbondale: Southern Illinois University Press, 1994); John E. Semonche, *Charting the Future: The Supreme Court Responds to a Changing Society, 1890-1920* (Westport, CN: Greenwood Press, 1978); John Henry Wigmore, *Evidence in Trials at Common Law*, revised by James H. Chadborn, 10 vols. (Boston: Little, Brown and Co., 1979); and G. Byron Dobbs, "Murder in the Supreme Court: Appeals from the Hanging

Judge," *Arkansas Law Review* 29 (Spring 1975): 47–70. Parker's suggestions for reforming the appellate system are found in his article "How to Arrest the Increase of Homicides in America," *North American Review* 162 (June 1896): 667–73.

For a thorough treatment of the source of one of the major disagreements between Parker and the Supreme Court, see Richard Maxwell Brown, *No Duty to Retreat: Violence and Values in American History and Society* (New York: Oxford University Press, 1991). See also two articles by Joseph H. Beale: "Homicide in Self-Defense," *Columbia Law Review* 3 (December 1903): 526–45, and "Retreat from a Murderous Assault," *Harvard Law Review* 16 (1902–1903): 567–82.

Essential for an understanding of the confusing political and legal status of the Indian Territory is Jeffrey Burton, *Indian Territory and the United States: Courts, Government, and the Movement for Oklahoma Statehood* (Norman: University of Oklahoma Press, 1995). Also helpful are Angie Debo, *And Still the Waters Run: The Betrayal of the Five Civilized Tribes* (Princeton, NJ: Princeton University Press, 1940) and her *The Road to Disappearance* (Norman: University of Oklahoma Press, 1941); Sidney L. Harring, *Crow Dog's Case: American Indian Sovereignty, Tribal Law, and United States Law in the Nineteenth Century* (New York: Cambridge University Press, 1996); H. Craig Miner, *The Corporation and the Indian: Tribal Sovereignty and Industrial Civilization in Indian Territory, 1865–1907* (Columbia: University of Missouri Press, 1976); Rennard Strickland, *Fire and the Spirits: Cherokee Law from Clan to Court* (Norman: University of Oklahoma Press, 1975); Mary Jane Warde, *George Washington Grayson and the Creek Nation* (Norman: University of Oklahoma Press, 1999); Murray R. Wickett, *Contested Territory: Whites, Native Americans, and African Americans in Oklahoma, 1865–1907* (Baton Rouge: Louisiana University Press, 2000); Jeanette W. Ford, "Federal Law Comes to Indian Territory," *Chronicles of Oklahoma* 58 (Winter 1980–81): 432–39;

Orville H. Platt, "Problems in Indian Territory," *North American Review* 160 (February 1895): 195–202; and Ken Peak, "Criminal Justice, Law, and Policy in Indian Country: A Historical Perspective," *Journal of Criminal Justice* 17 (1989): 393–407.

Among the more reliable works on the best-known defendant to appear before Parker are Glenn Shirley, *Belle Starr and Her Times: The Literature, the Facts, and the Legends* (Norman: University of Oklahoma Press, 1982); and Glenda Riley, "Belle Starr, 'Queen of the Bandits,'" in *With Badges and Bullets: Lawmen and Outlaws in the Old West*, ed. Richard W. Etulain (Golden, CO: Fulcrum Publishing, 1999), 139–58. Belle's kinsman by marriage gives his jaundiced views on Parker and his juries in Henry Starr, *Life of Henry Starr* (1914; reprinted in Carl W. Breihan and Charles A. Rosamond, *The Bandit Belle* [Seattle: Superior Publishing Co., 1970]).

Paul W. Keve, *Prisons and the American Conscience: A History of U.S. Federal Corrections* (Carbondale: Southern Illinois University Press, 1991) discusses the institutions to which Parker sent long-term prisoners. A database at the National Archives, Central Plains Region, Kansas City, Missouri, contains information about prisoners whom Parker sent from the Fort Smith court to the federal penitentiary in Leavenworth, Kansas.

Ed Bearss and Arrell M. Gibson, *Fort Smith: Little Gibraltar on the Arkansas* (Norman: University of Oklahoma Press, 1969) gives details on Parker and the community in which he held court. Other aspects of Fort Smith history are found in Carolyn Gray McMasters, *A Corner of the Tapestry: A History of the Jewish Experience in Arkansas, 1820s–1990s* (Fayetteville: University of Arkansas Press, 1994); and Ruth B. Mapes, *Old Fort Smith: Cultural Center on the Southwestern Frontier* (n.p.: 1965). A convenient source of state history is Carl H. Moneyhon, *Arkansas and the New South, 1874–1929* (Fayetteville: University of Arkansas Press, 1997). Useful facts about Parker's time in Missouri are in *The*

Daily News' History of Buchanan County and St. Joseph, Mo. From the Time of the Platte Purchase to the End of the Year 1898 (St. Joseph, MO: St. Joseph Publishing Co., 1898?).

Among the reference works I consulted were: *Encyclopedia of the American West*, 4 vols. (New York: Simon and Schuster Macmillan, 1996); Gerald T. Hanson and Carl H. Moneyhon, *Historical Atlas of Arkansas* (Norman: University of Oklahoma Press, 1989); *Index to Presidential Executive Orders and Proclamations. Part I: Apr. 30, 1789 to Mar. 4, 1921*, 10 vols. (Washington: Congressional Information Service, 1986); and John W. Morris and Edwin C. McReynolds, *Historical Atlas of Oklahoma* (Norman: University of Oklahoma Press, 1965).

Two novels by Douglas C. Jones featuring Parker as a character are especially worthwhile: *The Search for Temperance Moon* (New York: Henry Holt and Co., 1991); and *Winding Stair* (New York: Holt, Rinehart and Winston, 1979). Other works of fiction in which Parker appears are Larry McMurtry and Diana Ossana, *Zeke and Ned* (New York: Simon & Schuster, 1997); Charles Portis, *True Grit* (New York: Simon & Schuster, 1968) Elmer Kelton, *Hanging Judge* (New York: Ballantine, 1969); and David Freeman, *Jesse and the Bandit Queen: A Play in Two Acts* (New York: Samuel French, 1976). Richard Slotkin's engaging novel *The Return of Henry Starr* (New York: Atheneum, 1988) alludes to Parker. Reference works that led to information on novels and films relating to Parker include: *America in Historical Fiction: A Bibliographic Guide* (Englewood, CO: Libraries Unlimited, 1997) and Kevin Brownlow, *The War, the West, and the Wilderness* (New York: Alfred A. Knopf, 1979).

Index